John Reed

Twayne's United States Authors Series

Kenneth E. Eble, Editor
University of Utah

TUSAS 516

JOHN REED
(1887–1920)
Photograph reproduced courtesy of
Alfred A. Knopf, Inc.

John Reed

By David C. Duke

Marshall University

Twayne Publishers
A Division of G.K. Hall & Co. • *Boston*

John Reed

David C. Duke

Copyright © 1987 by G.K. Hall & Co.
All Rights Reserved
Published by Twayne Publishers
A Division of G.K. Hall & Co.
70 Lincoln Street
Boston, Massachusetts 02111

Copyediting supervised by Lewis DeSimone
Book production by Janet Zietowski
Book design by Barbara Anderson

Typeset in 11 pt. Garamond
by Modern Graphics, Inc., Weymouth, Massachusetts

Printed on permanent/durable acid-free paper and bound in the
United States of America

Library of Congress Cataloging in Publication Data

Duke, David C.
  John Reed.

  (Twayne's United States authors series ; TUSAS 516)
  Bibliography: p. 156
  Includes index.
  1. Reed, John, 1887–1920—Criticism and
interpretation. I. Title. II. Series.
PS3535.E2786Z68 1987   818'.5209   86–33542
ISBN 0-8057-7502-1

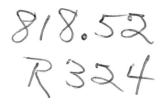
To Rainey, Marty, and Nathan

Contents

About the Author

David C. Duke is professor of history at Marshall University, Huntington, West Virginia. His interests are in American intellectual history and especially in writers as activists. He is the author of *Distant Obligations: Modern American Writers and Foreign Causes,* published by Oxford University Press.

Preface

John Reed's life is the substance of which legends are made. Before the age of thirty he had experienced more than most people do in a lifetime. Whether cavorting in Greenwich Village, being arrested in Paterson, riding with Pancho Villa, covering World War I, working with the Provincetown Players, writing for the *Masses,* engaging in tempestuous love affairs, or roaming the streets of revolutionary Petrograd, he was living an adventure. Little wonder that his contemporaries, whether they loved or hated him, mythologized his activities even before his death. While still alive, Reed was a character in a play and two novels, and was the subject of many stories and anecdotes.[1] After his death, both Communists and non-Communists claimed him as their own. In 1928, Soviet film director Sergei Eisenstein made a film of *Ten Days That Shook the World.* During the 1930s the American Communist party honored him by creating the John Reed clubs to attract young writers to radical causes. Ironically, over a quarter of a century later, when the 1956 Hungarian revolt shook the Communist world, James Michener's book *The Bridge at Andau* was billed as an on-the-spot description of "twelve days that shook the world."[2] Random House may have unintentionally parodied *Ten Days That Shook the World,* but Reed's book was still remembered well enough to strike a familiar chord.

The legend continues into our era. Perhaps no event or person is truly Americanized until made the subject of a Hollywood film. Warren Beatty's *Reds* further romanticized the lives and activities of Reed and Louise Bryant, while it cast doubts on their radicalism.[3] In 1982, Alan Cheuse published *The Bohemians,* the autobiographical novel that Reed had always hoped to write. As in the film, Reed's romantic entanglements greatly overshadow his politics.

In a life so filled with drama, commitments, and contradictions, it is little wonder that Reed has appeared so differently to so many people. This biographical diversity became apparent shortly after he left college. Fellow Harvard classmate Walter Lippmann evaluated his budding career for the *New Republic.* Emphasizing the playful side of Reed's personality, Lippmann described him as a kind of dilettantish chimera who, above all else, enjoyed life to its fullest. "He is many men at once, and those who have tried to bank on some phase of him, to regard him as a writer, a correspondent, a poet, a revolutionist, or a lover, lose him. There is no line between the play of his fancy and his responsibility to fact; he is for the time the person he imagines himself to be."[4] The legend of Reed as playboy was born. Albert Rhys Williams, who was a good friend and a fellow participant in the Bolshevik Revolution, saw Reed in an entirely different light. "The October Revolution made him a revolutionary. Poet, dramatist, and satirist, he saw the Revolution in all its spectacular aspects. His integrity demanded more, however: nothing less than an explanation of the seemingly blind forces at work—a quest that ended only with his death and martyrdom, making of him a legendary figure the world over, forever young and forever passionate, the twentieth century's Western creative man with a commitment."[5] Enter Reed the committed revolutionary.

Often overlooked in the Reed legend are his skills as a writer. In a ten-year career his publications included a book of verse, over two dozen stories and sketches, more than a hundred articles, half as many signed newspaper reports, several plays, and three books, among them *Insurgent Mexico* and his masterful *Ten Days That Shook the World*. This study is the first to examine Reed's literary career by focusing on the entire body of his writing. Yet there is no separating Reed's art from his life. His best writing always derived from events he had seen or participated in. In a moment of self-examination, he once suggested that "on the whole, ideas alone didn't mean much to me. I had to see. . . . It didn't come to me from books that the workers produced all the wealth of the world, which went to those who did not earn it."[6] Seeing also led to commitment and by the end of his life Reed was a devoted Communist. This sense of commitment ultimately exacerbated a tension that had always existed between his life and his career. Reed lived his life in a rush. Ambitious as well as inquisitive, he wanted to be at the center of everything he encountered whether it was college or Village life, the Paterson Pageant, or revolutionary turmoil. Paradoxically, participation both stimulated and threatened his creativity. He simply lacked the time to do all he intended, and once he started trying to change the world rather than just observe it, the tension between writing and doing became ever more apparent. At no time in his short life did Reed ever strike a balance between his need to write and his need to act. At no time was he able to apportion his energies comfortably between his work and his beliefs.

Since Reed's life and work are so closely tied, the first two chapters are devoted to a biographical sketch of his activities and commitments. In these chapters his works are discussed only insofar as they shed light on what he did. Chapters 3 through 6 examine his writing during four stages of his life, while chapter 7 attempts to evaluate his literary legacy.

David C. Duke

Marshall University

Acknowledgments

Grateful acknowledgment is made to the following publishers, institutions, and libraries:

The George Arents Research Library for Special Collections at Syracuse University for permission to quote material from the Granville Hicks Collection.

The Houghton Library of Harvard University at Cambridge for permission to quote material from the John Reed Papers.

The Morristown Archives of the Morristown-Beard School at Morristown for permission to quote material pertaining to John Reed.

The Harvard University Archives of Harvard University Library at Cambridge for permission to quote material by John Reed from the *Lampoon, Monthly,* and *Illustrated.*

The Collection of American Literature of the Beinecke Rare Book and Manuscript Library of Yale University at New Haven for the use of their copy of *Everymagazine: An Immorality Play.*

Random House, Inc. and Alfred A. Knopf, Inc. for use of the photograph from *Romantic Revolutionary: A Biography of John Reed* by Robert A. Rosenstone, copyright 1975.

This book could never have been completed without the generous assistance of many people. Professors Lee Erickson and Joan Adkins of the English department at Marshall University helped a historian evaluate Reed's poetry while my wife, Loraine, took time from her own busy career to assist with the short stories and sketches. Sara Wilson and Gwendolyn Canada in the Inter-Library Loan Department at Marshall University were tireless in tracking down obscure pieces of Reed's work. A special thanks also to the staffs at the Houghton Library and the Morristown Archives as well as to Carolyn A. Davis at the George Arents Research Library, Syracuse. I deeply appreciate Yvonne Tumblin's patience and professionalism in typing and retyping my manuscript. All Reed scholars are very much indebted to two masterful biographies: Granville Hicks's *John Reed: The Making of a Revolutionary* and Robert Rosenstone's *Romantic Revolutionary: A Biography of John Reed.* In addition, Rosenstone has gone far beyond the realm of scholarly generosity in helping me locate Reed-related materials and in offering other assistance. Above all, however, I must thank my colleague and friend Donna Spindel, who has read the manuscript more times than I care to recall. Her criticisms have been indispensable. The book has benefited immeasurably from the help of all these individuals, but I alone am responsible for its failings.

Finally I am grateful to Marshall University for the essential time (sabbatical and course reduction) and secretarial support that made this book possible.

Chronology

1887   John Silas Reed born 22 October, Portland, Oregon.

1893   Kidney problems begin.

1898   Enters school for first time: Portland Academy.

1904   Attends Morristown Academy, Morristown, New Jersey.

1906   Enters Harvard.

1910   Graduates from Harvard. Tours Europe.

1911   Returns from Europe; begins working for the *American* in New York. Moves to Greenwich Village in summer. Publishes first poems and stories.

1912   Begins association with the *Masses*.

1913   Publishes *The Day in Bohemia, or Life among the Artists* and *Everymagazine: An Immorality Play*. Directs Paterson Pageant. Spends summer in Europe with Mabel Dodge. Leaves in December for Mexico to cover Mexican Revolution for the *Metropolitan* and the New York *World*.

1914   Departs Mexico in March. In May reports on Ludlow Massacre. Leaves for Europe in August to cover World War I for the *Metropolitan* and the New York *World*.

1915   January, fires towards French lines from German trenches. Returns to United States end of January. Permanently barred from western front. Six-month tour of Eastern Europe.

1916   Publishes *The War in Eastern Europe*. Meets Louise Bryant in Portland and marries her that fall. Involved with Provincetown Players during summer. Kidney removed in November.

1917   Publishes *Tamburlaine*. Opposes American entry into war. Reporter for New York *Mail*. August, leaves for Russia with Bryant. Observes Bolshevik Revolution in November.

1918   February, leaves Petrograd but stranded in Christiana, Norway, until April because of State Department interference. September, defendant in second *Masses* trial. Publishes the *Sisson Documents*.

1919 Publishes *Ten Days That Shook the World.* Helps create American Communist Labor party. In September, leaves for Moscow to try to settle ideological disputes between American Communist factions.

1920 Leaves Russia in March for the United States. Arrested in Finland. Spends three months in solitary confinement in Finnish prison. Returns to Russia in June. July, participates in Second Congress of the Communist International. Attends Congress of Oriental Nations at Baku on the Caspian Sea in August. Reunited with Louise in Moscow in September. Dies of typhus in Moscow, 17 October.

Chapter One
Evolution of a Radical

By the spring of 1932, John Reed had been dead for almost twelve years, but the legend of his involvement in the Russian Revolution was still alive. At the height of the depression, when capitalism seemed at its nadir, the American Communist party sought to sustain the Reed legend by organizing the John Reed Club of New York. By 1932, there were a dozen such clubs. The members were dedicated to devoting their literary skills to worldwide revolutionary change. It was fitting that these radical literary organizations bore Reed's name, for this Harvard-educated poet, journalist, and adventurer had ardently devoted his own considerable talents to securing the revolution abroad and inspiring it at home.

Reed's mother, however, was appalled that the American Communist party had so honored her son. She considered it a smear on the family name and begged Lincoln Steffens, a friend and family advisor, to help get her son's name removed from these Communist literary organizations. Having known Reed for much of his short life, Steffens offered the mother little comfort. He assured her that her son had died for a cause in which he believed: "He became a hero in Russia; he will be for ages a Soviet Russian hero. And, Mrs. Reed," Steffens reiterated, "I'm afraid that you are wrong about his not standing for the use of his name by the clubs. My impression is that Jack would approve of that, or if he objected, he would have complained only that the John Reed Clubs do not go far enough. He might say to them what he said to me that night on a street corner in New York: "Go on—the limit.""[1]

Formative Years

Margaret Reed's dismay at the use of her son's name by a Communist organization reflected the social prominence of her family. Her father, a transplanted New Yorker, had carved both a fortune and a name for himself out of the rawness of the Pacific Northwest in the period before and immediately after the Civil War. Investing in furs and utilities, he moved to Portland, Oregon, only a decade after its founding. He prospered as the city grew and at his death in 1885 left behind a mansion, Cedar Hill, two sons and two daughters, and a widow, Charlotte Jones Green, who was every bit as independent and bold as her entrepreneur husband. Margaret Green shared little of her parent's independence. She attended finishing school in the East and then married a New York businessman who, like her father, had come to the Northwest to make his fortune.[2]

Charles Jerome Reed arrived at Portland as a representative of a company dealing in agricultural machinery. Known for his wit, charm, and intelligence, he soon became an important member of the business community. More a maverick than his socially prominent wife, C. J. Reed often chafed at the pretentiousness of Portland society and found little personal satisfaction in devoting his life to the acquisition of wealth. In 1905, he served as a United States marshall and helped to uncover land frauds in which thousands of acres of government timber had been illegally obtained by speculators. This venture into progressivism earned C. J. the friendship of Lincoln Steffens who reported on the scandal. It also earned him the enmity of the Portland business community. These people mistrusted any challenge to the status quo and especially disliked one of their own engaging in such unorthodox behavior as political reform. Snubbed by the Portland elite for his reforming venture, C. J. Reed never regained the prominence he had previously enjoyed.

John Silas Reed was born on 22 October 1887, a little less than a year after his parent's marriage, when they were still prominent in Portland social circles. Reed and his brother, Harry, two years his junior, were cared for by nurses at Cedar Hill, the serene home of their grandmother Charlotte Green. During this early period of their lives, both boys were influenced more by their mother's gentility than by their father's restlessness. In fact, there was little in Reed's youth to suggest his later activities.

A chronic kidney ailment, which plagued him for much of his life, contributed to the insularity of Reed's childhood. Treasured as a delicate child by his mother, Reed recalled that his early years were marked by frequent illness and a sense of physical weakness. Even more vivid in his memory was a belief that he was not living up to his father's expectations; he later expressed in an unpublished autobiographical essay, "Almost Thirty": "I wasn't much good at the things other boys were, and their codes of honor and conduct didn't hold me. . . . I was neither one thing nor the other, neither altogether coward nor brave, neither manly nor sissified, neither ashamed nor unashamed. . . . It must have disappointed my father that I was like that, though he never said much about it."[3]

Denied many of the more robust adventures of childhood, Reed discovered an imaginary world of his own by reading. The books he most enjoyed were predictably romantic: *Lorna Doone, The Arabian Nights, Tales of the Round Table,* and countless historical works that helped him to enliven the present with the past. A love of reading also stimulated his imaginative abilities and at the age of nine John decided that he wanted to be a writer. He and Harry also entertained one another and anyone else who would watch by building a theater in their attic and putting on plays written by John.[4]

The first school John attended was Portland Academy, which his parents believed more suitable than the public schools. Always somewhat of an indifferent student, he was more interested in the social than the academic aspects of life there. Although several teachers recognized Reed's writing skills, he does not appear to have used them as a means of social acceptance and advancement as he later did at prep school and in college. By his sixteenth birthday his health and confidence in himself had improved to the extent that he was more at ease with boys his own age and eager to participate in the usual outdoor activities of the Northwest. His parents were delighted by this newfound self-assurance and decided that the next two years should be spent in an eastern prep school where they believed John would be better prepared for college. Thus by the summer of 1904 John was not only preparing to leave behind the world of childhood, but also many of the anxieties that had haunted this early period. Over the next two years he underwent a remarkable social transformation. The old shyness and fears of physical weakness were replaced by a boisterous exuberance which became an enduring trait.

In the fall of 1906, John entered Morristown Academy in New Jersey where he remained for the next two years. Although it was not among the most prestigious of the eastern prep schools, the sixty-five boys who enrolled at Morristown came from decidedly upper-class backgrounds. The setting was pleasant with white framed buildings surrounded by ample lawns and playing fields. No longer the frail, shy introvert, Reed was outgoing and handsome with a tall, slender body offset by brown unruly hair, a broad forehead, large intense brown eyes, and an unmistakable pug nose over an often laughing mouth. Unlike his first, unpleasant days at Portland Academy, life at Morristown was far more reassuring. "Boarding school, I think, meant more to me than anything in my boyhood. Among these strange boys I came as a stranger, and I soon found out that they were willing to accept me at my own value" ("Almost Thirty" 132–33).

Fully in the mainstream rather than on the periphery of his environment, Jack, as he was then called, was often a leader in schoolboy horseplay; later one underclassman remembered him as a "King of the kids."[5] There were nights, for example, when he and others slipped down the dormitory fire escapes to attend local dances. At dawn the boys returned, exhausted and exhilarated. Reed courted the town girls arduously and then forgot them. Never feeling lonely, he seemed to have friends everywhere. As before, it was school activities rather than studies that most absorbed him. He played on the varsity football and track teams and won letters in each. He was also a member of the choir, pool club, and spring dance committee. More important for his later career, he quickly discovered that his writing, which he had always enjoyed, was also admired by others and could be used as an avenue for recognition. In 1905, he won a prize for the best historical essay and a year later won the school prize for poetry. In addition, he was a coeditor of the school yearbook and also served as one of four editors on the school newspaper, the *Morristonian*. Editing the paper not only gave him his first journalistic experience, it also allowed him to evaluate the work of others and to publish six short stories and a number of poems over a two-year period. John also believed that students had no outlet for humorous writing, and with his father's financial backing, he started and did much of the writing for the *Rooster*, a small newspaper that was intended to show the lighter side of life at Morristown. While Jack's father lent generous support, he found that so much extracurricular activity was hurting his son's grades. When the enterprise folded after several issues, C. J. acknowledged his relief to the headmaster: "I have been of the opinion that Jack would have none too much time for his studies this year and that he could not spare any to conduct the "Rooster" but as he seemed so absorbed in the paper and so proud of its record last year I did not have the heart to forbid his going on with it."[6]

Parental concern about Jack's activities interfering with his studies was justified. At the end of the second year, he managed only a C in English, D's in both history and French, a pass in chemistry, and failures in Latin and geometry. This left him eight points short for graduation. To make matters worse, he failed the Harvard entrance exams, which put his college career in jeopardy. But a summer's hard work with a tutor in Portland led to Reed's graduation from Morristown and entrance to Harvard in the fall of 1906. In a letter to Morristown about his younger son, C. J. showed that he was far from disappointed with the energetic but undisciplined older boy. Comparing John with his brother, Harry, he wrote: "Harry is much more serious and quiet than Jack and consequently will not get as much out of life but he will probably give you less trouble."[7] In addition to preparing him for college, the school enlarged the perimeters of his experiences and boosted his self-confidence as a person and a writer. The more staid atmosphere at Harvard did some initial damage to his ego, but in the long run, Reed's four years in Cambridge had a greater influence on him than the years spent at Morristown.

Harvard

Once at Harvard, Reed saw the intimacy of prep school life shattered by a large freshman class of seven hundred. The many friends he had enjoyed at Morristown gave way to loneliness. "I didn't know which way to turn, how to meet people. Fellows passed me in the Yard, shouting gayly to one another; I saw parties off to Boston Saturday night, whooping and yelling on the back platform of the streetcar, and they passed hilariously singing under my window in the early dawn" ("Almost Thirty" 133). Feeling excluded from campus life and bored by his studies, Reed sought acceptance and recognition through a flurry of activity. Trying the Morristown method, he went out for the freshman football team only to be cut within a few weeks. He devoted the rest of the fall and much of the winter to rigorous training for the freshman crew, but was assigned to the second team. It was only through writing that Reed enjoyed any success, mainly through his contributions to the bimonthly *Lampoon,* which gently satirized the university and attempted to portray the foibles of campus life humorously. Reed had more difficulty getting his work accepted by the *Harvard Monthly,* which was devoted to serious literary efforts. By the spring of his freshman year, however, this prestigious campus magazine accepted a poem and short story. Yet in spite of his literary accomplishments, Reed failed to gain entry to the inner circles of his class or to the elite social clubs whose members shared bonds of family, wealth, and eastern connections.

Reed's second year at Harvard was a considerable improvement over his first. A few months into the term he became a member of the varsity swimming and water polo teams. His writing went well. He continued to send jokes and humorous sketches to the *Lampoon* and several poems and stories to the *Monthly* and the *Harvard Advocate*. He was, in short, beginning to find acceptable channels for his considerable energies. He also made friends through the various campus organizations he had joined by the spring of 1908. The Cosmopolitan Club attracted students from around the world who met to discuss international problems and concerns. The Dramatic Club served as an outlet for budding playwrights to experiment with their work. In view of his later political activism, Reed's lack of interest in the Socialist Club is surprising. He attended several meetings when the club was formed in 1908, but played no important role.

Beginning midway through his sophomore year, Jack's campus activities increased at a frenzied pace. Writing continued to consume much of his time, and during his last two years at Harvard his poems and stories filled the pages of the *Lampoon,* the *Monthly,* and occasionally, the *Advocate* and the *Illustrated.* Always encouraged to write by his father and his teachers, Jack came to know during his junior year a professor who had a lasting influence on him. Charles Townsend Copeland, an assistant professor of English, was known more for his teaching—especially his English 12 class in composition—than for his scholarship. Copeland used unorthodox methods, often digressing from the subject matter to discuss an ever varying array of topics, all of which eventually returned to his primary concern: the writing of readable prose. He took special care with the work of his most capable undergraduate writers. Reed, who became one of his favorites, spent many Saturday evenings wedged with other students in Copeland's book-lined room where the topics of conversation were as varied as the participants. By his senior year Reed was among the select few who considered Copeland a friend.

Writing was not all that occupied Reed's time during his senior year. Ambitious with a tendency toward self-promotion, he engaged in a diversity of activities. As a cheerleader, on autumn afternoons, he unselfconsciously exhorted the student body to cheer the Crimson to victory. Years later Reed still recalled "the supreme blissful sensation of swaying two thousand voices in great clashing choruses during the big football games" ("Almost Thirty" 134–35). As second in command of the *Lampoon*, he wrote a regular column and editorials when time permitted. Reed continued to write for the *Monthly* and eventually served on its editorial board. President of the Cosmopolitan Club, he also regularly attended meetings of the Western Club, managed the Dramatic Club, and found time for the Glee, Mandolin and Guitar, and Banjo Clubs. Like a civic booster in a Sinclair Lewis novel, he was also a member of the Debating Club, Symposium, Round Table, and the Memorial Society.

All these activities fed Reed's ego while making him a well-known campus personality; ostensibly they also helped him forget the earlier snubs of Harvard's social elite. But under the surface, ironically, the same man who dedicated a portion of his life to revolutionary change, yearned as a college student for acceptance by the university's elitist social clubs. During a senior election controversy, for example, Reed sided with the campus aristocrats. Traditionally, the wealthier students lived in private apartments on Mount Saint Auburn Street while the rest of the student body occupied the more uncomfortable rooms in the yard. When the yard students challenged the customary domination of the senior elections by the Mount Saint Auburn Street clique, Reed sided with the latter. On another occasion, the elitist Hasty Pudding Club needed someone to write lyrics for its annual musical production. Having failed in the past to receive an invitation to join, Reed swallowed his pride and used his writing skills to serve his social ambitions. In short, John Reed, perhaps like most of his classmates, was a mixture of many conflicting traits by the end of his senior year. He was ambitious, self-promoting, and a bit unscrupulous. At the same time, Reed was outgoing, intelligent but not scholarly, boisterous, infectiously likable, and, above all else, eager to make his mark. Writing was one of the things that Reed did best. But before settling into a career he first wanted to see something of the world.

New York Apprenticeship

Indulgent parents once again assisted in Jack's desire to travel. When he and a classmate, Waldo Peirce, boarded a British cattle boat in July 1910 to work their way to Europe, it was with the understanding that Jack would try to earn his way but could expect financial help, if necessary. Immediately the voyage took on the proportions of an improbable college theatrical production when Peirce, who quickly became disenchanted with the prospects of attending cattle for two weeks, decided to return home several hours after the ship had sailed. Without telling anyone of his intentions, he slipped overboard and swam for home. Later discovering his friend's watch and wallet, Reed guessed what had happened. Knowing Peirce was a good swimmer, Reed was unconcerned. But an incredulous ship's captain, certain that Reed had murdered his companion, wired ahead informing the British authorities. Peirce relieved an embarrassing if not dangerous situation by catching a fast ship to England and dramatically entering the inquiry room where Reed was being questioned by the Board of Trade.[8] After this the trip settled into more conventional proportions with Jack limiting his travels to England, France, and Spain rather than the worldwide itinerary originally planned. "I'm busy learning French, reading and talking," he wrote to a college friend in October 1910, "and am trying out those magnificent talents which made the *Monthly* the talk of Cambridge when I was in college. For the present I have foresworn verse, following Cope's advice, and am buckling down to prose."[9] Apart from overdrawn descriptions of his travels in Spain, little remains of Reed's creative efforts, and after more than six months abroad he returned home in February 1911, with no works in progress but with memories of good times roaming about Europe.

Lincoln Steffens, whom Reed had met at Harvard, influenced the next phase of his life. Unlike Copeland, Steffens used the streets of New York to teach rather than the classroom. Reed first met Steffens when he spoke at Harvard; later he praised the muckraker's book *The Upbuilders* in a review for the *Monthly,* March 1910. Soon after Reed settled in New York during the winter of 1910–11 when he was trying to sharpen his writing skills, his father wrote to Steffens, a friend, and asked him to help his son. "Get him a job, let him see everything, but don't let him be anything for a while," C. J. pleaded. "Don't let him get a conviction right away or a business or a career, like me. Let him play." Steffens found a job for the young writer on the *American Magazine,* but he first made Jack promise to treat his position as "a springboard from which to dive into life"—rather than as a career to be pursued.[10] He also suggested to the recent Harvard graduate that city life itself had much to teach him.

Thus in the summer of 1911 Reed and three former Harvard classmates moved into a third-floor, walk-up apartment at 42 Washington Square South. Work on the *American Magazine* proved to be relatively undemanding: Reed corrected proof, read manuscripts, and eventually helped to put the magazine together.[11] With plenty of free time, John followed Steffen's advice and began to explore the city with the appetite of the starved. "New York was an enchanted city to me. It was on an infinitely greater scale than Harvard. Everything was to be found there—it satisfied me utterly" ("Almost Thirty" 138). The east side seemed more exciting than Europe; he wandered its pushcart-crowded streets, listened to its babble of languages, and observed the hordes of newcomers who seemed as awed as he. It was unlike any world he had known and his senses were overwhelmed with the thrill of new experiences.

In his wanderings through the city Reed was developing a talent so evident in much of his later work: the ability to describe vividly what he saw. His enthusiasm for the city soon spilled over into his writing and unlike the young Jack London who struggled for years to get published, Reed's period of famine was relatively short. Earlier he had collaborated with a more established writer to publish the Waldo Peirce shipboard escapade in the *Saturday Evening Post,* 28 October 1911. By mid-1912, several of his poems and articles had appeared in *Century, American, Collier's, Trend,* and *Forum.* The *American* commissioned him to do a long study, never published, of the intellectual upheaval at Harvard during his last two years there.[12] Cheered by his successes, Reed often discussed his future plans with Lincoln Steffens, who had moved into a room below Reed and his friends. Visiting Steffens at all hours of the day and night, the exuberant Reed delighted the older journalist: "I used to go early to bed and to sleep, but I liked it when Jack, a big, growing, happy being, would slam into my room and wake me up to tell me about the 'most wonderful thing in the world' that he had seen, been, or done that night." As a fellow writer and observer, Steffens appreciated Reed's animated descriptions of "girls, plays, bums, I.W.W.'s, strikers—each experience was vivid in him, a story, which he often wrote; every person, every idea."[13]

Reed worked for an established magazine in uptown Manhattan, but he spent much of the time in Greenwich Village, a geographical

location and a frame of mind. It was located downtown but surrounded by the city like a clearing in a forest. The well-to-do had
long since abandoned the Village's narrow, irregular streets. Spa-
cious but rundown buildings were now occupied by immigrants
(largely Italian), artists, and writers attracted by cheap rents, cheap
restaurants, and a convivial atmosphere. By the time Reed moved
there in the summer of 1911, an American bohemia was already
emerging. In many respects the Village offered the kind of atmosphere that Reed had sought at Harvard, for its toleration of the
unusual—the offbeat—went beyond the norms of "good form." To
be accepted, there were no traditions he had to follow. Most important of all, as one young writer observed, "it was more, and less,
than a place where people were free to 'be themselves.' It was,
among other things, very conspicuously to an intruder, a place where
people came to solve some of their life problems."[14]

At this time in his life Reed's most serious problem seemed to
be his excess energy. This became most apparent when his association
with the *Masses* began in December 1912. Originally a cooperative
endeavor, the *Masses* was reorganized in 1912 with the appointment
of Max Eastman as its first full-time editor. Eastman abandoned a
doctoral thesis at Columbia University to take the job, which included dealing with unrestrained personalities like Reed's. Their
first meeting was not promising. Reed rushed into Eastman's office,
thrust a story into the new editor's hands, and then refused to remain
seated during their entire conversation. "He stood up or moved
about the room all through his visit and kept looking in every
direction except that in which he was addressing his words," Eastman wrote some years later. "It is difficult for me to get the sense
of togetherness with a stranger, even if he looks at me. And when
he looks at the walls or the house fronts on the other side of the
street, and talks into the air, and walks around in this excessively
steamed-up manner, I am hopelessly embarrassed and want to lie
down and rest after it is over." Instead of resting, however, Eastman
read Reed's story, "Where the Heart Is" about a prostitute who
takes an extensive vacation abroad before realizing that she is hap-
piest when working in her old saloon in New York. Eastman forgot
his initial qualms, knowing that he had just met "a man writing
about a significant phase of American life that no other magazine
would dare to mention unless sanctimoniously, and writing with
unlabored grace—a style both vivid and restrained."[15] A short time

later Reed was elected to the editorial board of the magazine that best captured the intellectual, cultural, and political flowering of the pre–World War I Village. At its best, the *Masses* was experimental, daring, clever, and openly disdainful of Victorian culture and the cant of middle-class values. Anticipating many of the concerns of the 1930s, the magazine frequently contained discussions on the relationship between art and politics, written in a fresh and challenging style. Reed soon came to know well Eastman and his assistant editor, Floyd Dell, as well as other members of the staff—Louis Untermeyer, Mary Heaton Vorse, Art Young, John Sloan, Boardman Robinson, and Robert Minor. Encouraged by the socialist views of many of these individuals, Reed began to read radical literature and to attend socialist meetings. Most of all, however, he enjoyed himself thoroughly while flourishing at the center of Village life.[16]

The only tragic note during these idyllic years was the death of C. J. Reed in 1912. Jack became determined never to be drawn under by the kind of pressures he believed had killed his father. Voicing the antibourgeois sentiments of the Village, he wrote to a college friend: "My father worried himself to death, that's all. He never let any of us know, but he was harassed into the grave. Money!"[17]

Reed's success as an author continued into 1913. The appearance of his articles in such commercial magazines as the *American* and the *Metropolitan* allowed him the luxury of sending more experimental or radical pieces to the *Masses*. Reed clearly enjoyed the role of writer and remained comfortable with his unconventional existence. In 1913, he wrote a gentle parody of Village life that to a lesser extent did for his generation what Jack Kerouac's *On the Road* did for a later one. *The Day in Bohemia, or Life among the Artists* was Reed's most sustained poetic effort to that point and demonstrated his joie de vivre, his serious commitment to his work, and his ability to poke fun at the very things in which he was most involved.

During this happy period of his life, Reed spent time at a well-known Village institution—the salon of Mabel Dodge. The daughter of a wealthy banker, she had lived for nine years with her second husband, the architect Edwin Dodge, in a palatial villa in Florence. When this marriage began to deteriorate, Dodge returned to New York in 1912 and rented an apartment at 23 Fifth Avenue on the border of the Village. Physically striking with a roundish face and bobbed hair, Dodge was also a good listener, receptive to innovative ideas. Her apartment with its white decor and antique furnishings soon became a gathering place for a wide assortment of people who enjoyed the eclectic atmosphere as well as the food and drink lavishly provided by their hostess. "Everybody in the ferment of ideas could be found there," according to Max Eastman, including Walter Lippmann, Lincoln Steffens, Hutchins Hapgood, Bernard Berenson, Carl Van Vechten, Andrew Dasburg, and Gertrude Stein.[18] Besides artists and writers, Dodge also attracted anarchists, socialists, and members of the iww. With his boundless energy and nose for excitement, Reed inevitably discovered her salon.

Romantic Journalist

While attending a Village gathering in the early spring of 1913, Reed became enthralled by the one-eyed organizer of the Industrial Workers of the World (iww), Bill Haywood, as he described an ongoing strike of immigrant silk-workers in nearby Paterson, New Jersey. A labor victory in an iww-led strike in Lawrence, Massachusetts, the previous year had encouraged the Paterson workers, who faced a speeded-up work day and deplorable working conditions, to leave their looms in late February 1913. Haywood described how the owners, local government officials, and the press were all aligned against the strikers. Reed decided to go to Paterson to see for himself.

Initiation into the realities of class war began for Reed on a rainy April morning when he arrived in the dingy New Jersey city. Watching as the local police tried to clear the streets of strikers, he sought shelter from the rain under a porch roof only to be told to move on by a policeman who was swinging a billy club. Demanding that he be arrested if he were breaking a law, Reed was granted his request. An unsympathetic magistrate sentenced him to twenty days in the local jail. When they were assured that he was not a police spy, Reed's fellow prisoners gradually accepted him. Most of them, including Bill Haywood, were either strikers or iww organizers. As he listened to stories of past wrongs and joined in the singing of iww songs, Reed became converted and emerged from his four days in jail fully committed to the workers' cause. He also emerged with a new respect for the camaraderie and dedication of the iww members. Yet underlying his commitment to the wrongs suffered by the strikers was a sense of enjoyment of being part of a grand adventure. "If you saw the strikers in here," he wrote to a Harvard classmate who had originally gone to Paterson with him, "you would realize that it is a *great strike.* Unfortunately, perhaps, my infernal sense of Romance and Humor makes me rather enjoy it."[19] The former inmate became something of a Village hero as word of his incarceration spread. When Hutchins Hapgood, his wife, and Mabel Dodge drove to Paterson shortly after Reed's release, they were amazed by what they found. Arriving in the midst of a mass meeting, they discovered Reed on a balcony, leading the workers in strike songs.[20] He might have been leading cheers at a Harvard football game. Yet the Paterson strike was not just another adventure for Reed. The workers had shown him a kind of mass courage he had never known. When he reported on the strike a short time later ("War in Paterson," *Masses,* June 1913) he wrote as a participant, not as a neutral observer—a participant who for the first time believed in his cause. Reed's belief was such, in fact, that he was no longer content to support the striking workers with his pen, and he was soon involved in one of the strike's most colorful and remembered moments—the Paterson Pageant.

Who originally thought of organizing a pageant is not known, but Reed worked more than anyone to make the plan a reality.[21] He took on the responsibilities of writing a scenario and directing the production. Two Harvard classmates lent their support—Bobby Jones designed the stage set and Eddy Hunt served as Reed's special assistant. John Sloan from the *Masses* staff promised to paint scenery. In spite of other voluntary efforts Reed still faced a monumental task. He planned to reenact the strike with the workers playing the dominant role on stage. Reed rented a union hall and directed the rehearsals. Indifferent to his youth or lack of experience in labor disputes, Jack was everywhere giving instructions, asking questions, offering suggestions, pleading, encouraging, and often doing without food or sleep.

The day of the pageant, 7 June, began spectacularly; thousands of strikers arrived in New York and marched up Fifth Avenue carrying red banners. An IWW band joined them, playing the "Marseillaise" and the "International." Madison Square Garden was rented for the production. That evening ten-foot-high, lighted letters IWW glittered from the Garden's roof like a lighthouse beacon to the city. The only snag was that while the cheaper seats quickly filled, the more expensive floor seats did not. To fill the house, all remaining seats were either sold for fifty cents or simply given away to the milling crowd outside.

The pageant was an artistic success and a financial failure. As workers' theater, it was brilliant; the first of six scenes opened with subdued workers trudging to work, and them coming to life as they shut the mills down and begin to strike. Remaining scenes dramatized the funeral of a slain worker, a Sunday mass meeting, and the much publicized tactic of insulating strikers' children from the strike by sending them outside the city to sympathetic families. Reed set the final scene in a union hall and concluded the program with speeches by IWW leaders Carlos Tresca, Patrick Quinlan, Elizabeth Gurley Flynn, and Bill Haywood. They asked the audience to show its solidarity by standing and singing the "International" with the cast.[22]

Reed and the other sponsors of the pageant hoped that it would gain political support for the strike and raise six thousand dollars for the strikers. A deficit resulted instead. Too many free tickets and a too costly production had diminished receipts. Elizabeth Gurley Flynn claimed that the financial failure of the pageant and the misplaced energies in producing it left the workers disillusioned and contributed to the strike's ultimate failure.[23] Reed had done everything possible to make the pageant a success. Yet its failure haunted him for years, and perhaps, helps to explain his eventual commitment to a revolution in which workers depended only on themselves. His most immediate reaction, however, was to allow one of his coworkers, through her considerable charms, to lure him to Europe.

Reed and Mabel Dodge had discovered one another shortly after he got out of jail. Their infatuation grew as they worked together during the whirlwind days before the pageant. The day after the pageant, before recriminations had begun and the full scale of the financial disaster was known, Dodge and several friends sailed for Europe where they planned to spend the summer in her villa outside Florence. Eight years older than Reed, Dodge hoped to channel some of his energies toward her. The Villa Curonia was to be her testing ground. Reed was happy to be back in Europe. Dodge was but one of his diversions, and his distractions angered her. She recorded in her intimate memoirs: "I hated to see him interested in Things. I wasn't, and didn't like to have him even look at churches and leave me out out of his attention."[24] Reed, on the other hand, found Europe and life at the villa completely to his liking. As he explained to his friend Eddy Hunt: "I really haven't done any work at all here. One simply can't—there are so many new impressions to take in."[25] Despite the conflict between Dodge's possessiveness and Reed's interest in the outside world, the summer of 1913 was a fascinating one for both. They decided to live together in Dodge's apartment on Fifth Avenue when they returned to New York in the fall. But the relationship, in fact, was doomed. If Mabel could not dominate Jack's attentions in the luxury of her Italian villa, she certainly could not do so in New York. Back in New York Reed was restless and eager to work, while Mabel felt increasingly left out of his life. Their relationship faltered even more when the *Metropolitan* magazine, on Lincoln Steffens' recommendation, asked Reed to cover the Mexican Revolution. Reed accepted at once. His reporting of the events in Mexico had a major impact on his life. Within a few months he was transformed from a free-lance writer and Village personality, to one of the best-known and most sought after journalists in America. As had happened in Paterson, Reed not only reported a cause in Mexico, but became committed to it. Some of his best and most vivid prose emerged from this experience.

The Mexican Revolution began in the spring of 1911 with the overthrow of the corrupt and foreign-dominated government of General Porfirio Diaz by a conservative reformer, Francisco Madero. One of the generals of the rebellion, Victoriano Huerta, soon overthrew Madero. With the revolution in jeopardy, the struggle continued. Emiliano Zapata, the Indian revolutionary, led the opposition to Huerta in the South. Zapata sought land reform, a goal shared by the ex-cowboy and bandit, Pancho Villa, whose forces controlled the large, northern state of Chihuahua. Besides Zapata and Villa, Huerta's opposition also included Venustiano Carranza, governor of the state of Coahuila. Carranza sought political rather than social reform while considering himself the rightful heir of Madero.

Interpreting the situation in Mexico would have challenged the abilities of a veteran State Department official. Reed was a young reporter who knew little Spanish and had no experience in political journalism. If he had any doubts they were short-lived, for by December 1913, he was on his way to Mexico. On an impulse Dodge joined him in Chicago. According to Reed's version of their journey to El Paso, the two made an improbable pair. Wearing a bright corduroy suit himself, Reed describes how Dodge appeared in a "bright orange sweater (she also had a crimson one and an Alice blue one for the campaign),—whereupon two Mexicans became epileptic out of sheer covetousness, and an Indian had hysterics." Jack may not have known what he would find in Mexico, but he wrote that Mabel "expects to find General Villa a sort of male Gertrude Stein,—or at least a Mexican Stieglitz."[26]

Arriving in El Paso, Reed found the city to be a virtual aviary of intrigue. After several days of roaming about and listening to contradictory stories about the revolution, he was anxious to get into Mexico to see for himself. After traveling two hundred miles to the little Texas border town of Presidio, he managed to cross over into Ojinaga. There the remnants of a federal army were hovering after their defeat a month earlier by the Villastas. Reed interviewed the nervous commander, and then returned to El Paso where he found Dodge bored with waiting for him and thoroughly disgruntled with their shabby accommodations. When she abruptly returned to New York, Reed immediately plunged back into Mexico and the fascinating intrigues of violent social upheaval. For the next three months his adventures bordered on the surreal. He interviewed Pancho Villa, Carranza, generals, common soldiers, peasants, and American capitalists, all the while experiencing the brutalities of war. Several times he came close to death, but never allowed danger or inconvenience to lessen his growing admiration for the land and its people. Reed traveled throughout Chihauhua and Durango to see as much of the fighting as possible. Until they were routed by federal troops, he rode with a small contingent of Villastas. Later he was with Villa's army during its advance on Torreón, the last military obstacle between the Villastas and Mexico City. While riding, living, singing, and drinking with those tough and volatile soldiers, Reed found a camaraderie somewhat like the IWW spirit he had encountered in the Paterson jail. Reed was most impressed by Pancho Villa. Unlike Carranza, who he found to be aloof and withdrawn from the realities of daily events, Pancho Villa was a folk hero who seemed to be everywhere. Reed's dispatches and later his book were filled with anecdotes about Villa—helping to load horses into boxcars, dancing for two solid days and nights before a major battle, and personally attending to his own roosters in the cockpit. On the other hand, Villa liked the young American and allowed him privileges denied other journalists. It is thus not surprising that Reed overlooked atrocities committed by the Villastas or that he overestimated Villa's military skills. Still, Villa was something more than a colorful personality to be sketched and then forgotten. Much like Bill Haywood, he was the embodiment of social change. He symbolized for Reed a leader who was so closely tied to his followers that separating the aspirations of the two was unthinkable.

As Reed's reporting on the Mexican Revolution was published in the United States, he became widely known. Brilliant articles appeared in the *Metropolitan* while shorter reports were sent to the New York *World*. His adventures were the stuff of legends. What Stephen Crane and Richard Harding Davis had done for the Spanish-American War, Reed was doing for the Mexican Revolution. His youth added glamour to his exploits while his writing skills made the revolution come alive. When he returned to New York in the spring of 1914, he continued to send his Mexican articles to the *Metropolitan*. After several months of editing, selecting, and adding material already published, he completed his first major book, *Insurgent Mexico*. This work discussed the revolution from the viewpoint of an insider, one who shared its dangers and exhilarated in its ideals. Like the inextricable ties Reed described between Villa and his men, so were his own sense of commitment and his writing united. Reed emerged from Mexico more socially aware than previously, and his next journalistic assignment added to his growing consciousness.

While Reed was still enjoying his accomplishments as a war correspondent and writing articles describing the Mexican Revolution, a five-month strike in the southern Colorado coal fields was reaching its bloody conclusion. In late 1913, a group from the United Mine Workers had gone into the Trinidad district to organize miners of the Rockefeller-owned Colorado Fuel and Iron Company. Predictably state and local officials opposed the organizers. After the strike was called, participating miners were evicted from company houses. Many of the miners then moved their families into union-sponsored tent colonies in the surrounding valleys. The largest was at Ludlow. There on 20 April 1914 a contingent of state militia and the company deputies opened fire on the colony and burned it. Among the dead were two women and eleven children who had suffocated while hiding in protective pits beneath the tents. Their deaths led to a week-long battle between the militia and enraged miners. Finally, the Wilson administration sent in federal troops to ensure peace. Reed arrived in Colorado in the aftermath of the battle, and there was little doubt where his sympathies lay. He spoke at meetings for miners' relief, and served on a committee with George Creel and Judge Ben Lindsay to help win national recognition for the strikers.[27] He also wrote a long, detailed article, "The Colorado War" (*Metropolian,* July 1914), which was more somber and angry in tone than anything he had done in Mexico. As in Paterson, he found all the power aimed against the strikers. This experience affected him similarly to his involvement in Paterson and in Mexico; he became more radical because of what he saw and knew firsthand.

World War I

It was not long after the Ludlow Strike that another event contributed to Reed's growing radicalism—the shattering of worldwide working-class solidarity with the outbreak of World War I. When the guns of August began their destructive roar in the summer of 1914, Reed's reputation as a war correspondent was at its height. The *Metropolitan* had sent him to Ludlow with the claim "When there is war, John Reed is the writer to describe it." The magazine also carried an advertisement for the Corona folding typewriter, showing a picture of Reed at the keys with the reminder that the little machine could be easily carried into the thick of the fray.[28] Both the *Metropolitan* and the New York *World* eagerly sent Reed to Europe. But he soon found that the war was far different from the one in Mexico, and getting into the fray was far more difficult than he had expected.

Reed held nationalism in contempt as a justification for war and suspected that there were also deep-seated commercial causes for the conflict. But once the fighting began, he wanted to see as much of it as possible. Expecting Italy to enter the war as a Central Power, Reed sailed in August for Naples. Mabel Dodge met him there and was again prepared to follow him. Learning that German armies were racing towards Paris, they hurriedly departed for the French capital. Once in Paris, Reed tried to reach the front. From the start the war was difficult for him to understand. He wondered why workers, peasants, and common soldiers on all sides willingly marched off to be slaughtered for ill-defined objectives. He found none of the sense of purpose shown by the Villastas, who believed they were constructing a future for themselves and their children. As a result, the sense of commitment to a shared cause that had electrified his writing about Paterson, Mexico, and Ludlow was missing in Europe. He tried to substitute for it a kind of artificial excitement over his personal efforts to avoid the military red tape that discouraged journalists from reaching the front. In Paris, for example, he and fellow journalist Robert Dunn tried to get to the front lines by obtaining a car and a false medical excuse. Caught by French military authorities, they were told they faced imprisonment and expulsion from France if their persistence continued. Reed then went to London, which he found even more depressing and difficult to understand than Paris. Tired of his absences, Dodge abandoned him once again. To his dismay Reed also found that he could not write well about a war he hated and of which he could not be a part. Hoping that access to the front would be available elsewhere, he arranged to go to Germany. There he met Dunn and the two engaged in yet another prank that ended their hopes of covering the western front. On a rainy January evening in 1915 they were allowed into the front lines where they finally experienced the mud, boredom, and horrors of trench warfare. When a German officer casually suggested that the two reporters might enjoy firing toward the enemy, both Reed and Dunn accepted the invitation, each sending a shot in the general direction of the French lines. Dunn foolishly reported the incident in an article several weeks later. Outraged British and French authorities permanently barred Dunn and Reed from their sectors.[29] Reed returned to New York in the spring of 1915, met by little of the fanfare that had welcomed him back from Mexico. His reputation as a war correspondent was tarnished and his anger about the madness of the war was growing.

Reed's editors on the *Metropolitan* were appalled to find their star reporter on the sidelines, barred from the war zones. For his part, Reed was restless and concerned about his writing. Two months later, the *Metropolitan* decided to send him back to Europe. This time he was to be joined by an artist-illustrator, Boardman Robinson, and they were to go through the Balkans and into Russia to report on the war in the East. The two were well suited for one another, and their adventures on this six-month journey through Eastern Europe rivaled many of Reed's in Mexico. Reed found the war in the East more accessible and he could use his senses and his descriptive skills, which had served him so well in Mexico. But there was a difference. Horrified by the war's senseless waste, he could not identify with it. His travels in Serbia, for example, reinforced his hatred for the war. There he saw an entire nation devastated, with its thousands of dead and mutilated soldiers, villages ravaged by bombardment and typhus, and fields left untended by a demoralized population. But to his utter amazement, the people showed no bitterness. Their nationalism blinded them to the enormity of the disaster. As in Mexico, heroism and courage he found in abundance, but in Serbia it all seemed for nothing.

After leaving the Balkans, Reed and Robinson tackled a far more difficult task—reaching the Russian front. In spite of the dangers they faced, their attempts to travel towards the fighting in Russia had a ludicrous cast. Imperial officials often stopped them, annoyed that they had been allowed to travel so far in forbidden areas. Then, inexplicably, they would give the travelers written permission to proceed on to the next city, thus verifying the legality of their activities. In spite of their amazing good luck and their own audacity, Reed and Robinson failed to reach the front. They were arrested and imprisoned for two weeks in a hotel in the ancient city of Cholm. Released and sent to Saint Petersburg, they endured continuing harassment. Finally, exasperated imperial officals abruptly ordered them out of Russia in the late summer of 1915. Reed and Robinson traveled two months more through the Balkans in search of copy. Reed eventually went off on his own for a short visit to Turkey in another unsuccessful effort to reach the front. He then returned to New York, eager to write about his experiences. During his travels he supplied a number of articles to the *Metropolitan* and in 1916 published a book based on these articles entitled *The War in Eastern Europe*.

In 1916, Reed's life took quite a different turn. He had fallen in love with a young woman he had met in Portland late in the previous year. Reed's relationship with Dodge had never kept him from casual affairs and neither permanence nor fidelity were enduring parts of his personality. But after meeting this slender, black-haired, green-eyed wife of a dentist, Reed had found the person with whom he would share the rest of his life. Louise Bryant also thought of herself as a writer, although her enthusiasm and ambitions were somewhat larger than her abilities. Bored with Portland and a conventional marriage, she was ready for a change. Within several weeks of their first meeting, the two were sharing Reed's Village apartment, and in the fall of 1916 they married. The relationship was unconventional, tempestuous, passionate, filled with competition, professional jealousies, infidelities on both sides, and genuine affection. There was something naively courageous about it as well. As Max Eastman recalled, the two seemed determined "to smash through the hulls of custom and tradition and all polite and proper forms of behavior, and touch at all times and all over the earth the raw current of life. It was a companionship in what philistines call adventure, a kind of gypsy compact."[30]

As the relationship between the two deepened, they seemed to distance themselves from the war. In the early summer of 1916 they became part of one of the most original efforts ever undertaken to transform the American theater. The site of the project was Provincetown, a sleepy, seaside village in Massachusetts that had become a mecca for writers and artists. Among them was George Cram Cook, a writer and self-styled Hellenist, and his writer wife, Susan Glaspell. Cook disliked the commercialism and conservatism of the New York stage. He hoped to revitalize the American drama by introducing the innovative vitality of the ancient Greek plays, which he believed had so sharply mirrored the values of their time and society. Reed was soon an energetic partner. He had always had a deep interest in drama, for besides his dramatic efforts at Harvard and in the Paterson Pageant, he had written a number of plays that had not been produced. Using a wharf provided by writer and Provincetown resident Mary Heaton Vorse, Cook built a small theater with the sea as background. In their first summer the Provincetown Players put on four one-act plays. Reed and Bryant were soon directly involved—helping with the staging, acting in various productions, writing their own plays. Reed's play *Freedom* was included in the Players' first bill and Bryant's *The Game* was done at a later date. The discovery of Eugene O'Neill and the production of his *Bound East for Cardiff* ensured that summer's success and established the lasting fame of the Provincetown Players. It also provided an interesting diversion for Louise, who, unknown to Jack, began an affair with O'Neill that lasted over the next two years.

Just how aware Reed was of the growing attraction between Bryant and O'Neill is unknown, for by midsummer of 1916 he was being pulled in a number of different directions that were absorbing most of his energies.[31] In addition to his work with the Provincetown

Players, he was turning his attention to the preparedness movement
that was sweeping the country. In an article he wrote in July for
the *Masses* ("At the Throat of the Republic," July 1916), he lashed
out at the forces he believed were trying to stampede America into
war. A short time later he expressed his fears ("Whose War?" *Masses,*
April 1917) that Wall Street, munitions manufacturers, and other
war-related industries were insidiously nudging the country towards
a conflict whose destructive potential was far greater than most
Americans realized. Having seen the deadly impact of the war on
other countries, Reed believed that the only sane choice for the
United States was to remain aloof from the organized madness of
the conflict.

Reed supported the Democrats in the campaign of 1916, hoping
that they would carry out their promise of American neutrality. By
the beginning of 1917, he began to question the motives of the
reelected president. When the United States officially entered World
War I, many of Reed's worst fears about life in wartime America
were realized. A short time after the formal declaration of war, he
was in Washington testifying before a House Committee on Military
Affairs. Claiming that he was not a pacifist, he reiterated that he
was merely opposed to fighting in the present war. "I just think
that it is unjust on both sides," he proclaimed in his testimony,
"that Europe is mad, and that we should keep out of it."[32] Controversial views were not welcome in a society that was patriotically
closing ranks. Many journals that earlier had competed for Reed's
articles now rejected the work of an antiwar radical, and he found
it increasingly difficult to get his work in print. Desperate for funds,
he agreed to write a daily column for the *New York Mail,* a newspaper
that was less shrilly patriotic than most. He wrote for the *Mail* from
late May to August 1917, while continuing to send his more controversial articles to the *Masses.* But this magazine's criticism of
wartime America led to its prohibition from newsstands in New
York City subways, loss of contracts with magazine distributors,
and to harassment by the federal government. Reed had earlier
predicted much of what was happening, and in September 1917,
he somberly concluded that the month just past had seen the beginning of a frontal attack on democratic liberties. "With a sort of
hideous apathy the country has acquiesced in a regime of judicial
tyranny, bureaucratic suppression and industrial barbarism, which

followed inevitably the first fine careless rapture of militarism" ("One Solid Month of Liberty," *Masses*, September 1917, 5).

As wartime hysteria increased, Reed learned for the first time what it meant to suffer for his convictions. He had seen men and women die for their revolutionary beliefs, the hungry families of striking workers, and the charred remains of the Ludlow tent colony. In reporting these scenes he had identified with the oppressed, personally supporting their causes. But he had never truly been a part of the events. Now, because of his antiwar stance, Reed's career was in jeopardy. When the federal government finally suppressed the *Masses* in December 1917, even that vehicle for his writing was gone. While Reed's suffering was relatively minor, he was still learning firsthand what it meant to hold an unpopular view. But he did not waver. In fact, his observation of the monolithic powers of the wartime state made him even more radical. No longer the boisterous campus personality leading thousands in rousing cheers for the hometeam, Reed was in 1917 perceived by many as a dangerous subversive whose opinions should be silenced.

"Almost Thirty"

Reed's concern about the drift of the country was not all that disrupted his life. Personal concerns also intervened. The kidney problem that had plagued his childhood and reoccurred in adult years became so serious that in the fall of 1916, he needed an operation. Traveling to Baltimore alone, he entered Johns Hopkins where physicians removed his left kidney. Although the operation was successful, for a man used to robust physical activity the long period of recovery was difficult. Shortly before the operation Reed and Bryant had married for the purely practical purpose of insuring that she would be Reed's legal heir if he died. In spite of marriage, their relationship, like Reed's health, was in a period of decline. They were deeply attracted to one another and often depended on one another for emotional support, yet both continued to have affairs. Bryant was still involved with O'Neill, and although Reed was by then aware of the relationship, he was probably ignorant of its length and depth.[33] Reed, on the other hand, was more casually promiscuous. Yet his infidelities enraged Bryant who confronted him with bitter accusations. As the marriage declined, Reed helped his wife to obtain a job with the Wheeler News Syndicate to report on the war from Paris. When she left New York in June 1917, neither knew how long the separation would be. Two days after Louise sailed, Jack wrote to her in a reflectively apologetic tone: "Got here to find your pitiful little note—it isn't you who must learn, my honey, but me. In lots of ways we are very different, and we must both try to realize that—while loving each other." Old, familiar haunts brought painful memories, and he concluded: "I got into town at two this morning, and walked around the streets until almost dawn, thinking of my darling and of everything. It is really quite frightfully lonely without you. But I think the very loneliness will drive me to work, and I may get something done."[34]

Reed hoped, in fact, to use a tactic that had served him well in the past—to avoid personal problems by burying himself in his work. But he found that for the first time in his life he was simply unable to write. He complained to Louise in a letter of late June: "I am certainly very disoriented, without much pep or ambition this summer. The war, I suppose, and the heat."[35] A few weeks later his condition had not improved. "I do hope I can get to feeling like writing again. I seem to be entirely out of it."[36] Although not yet thirty, Reed's illness, his disillusionment with the war, and his troubled marriage made him feel suddenly old. He confided to Louise: "I am finding out things about myself, dearest in all this loneliness: I have discovered with a shock, how far I have fallen from the ardent young poet who wrote about Mexico."[37] But in fact, Reed had described many of these same feelings at an earlier time. In his only attempt at autobiography, he had written an unpublished essay entitled "Almost Thirty." Reed began that piece by speculating that an important part of his life was forever behind him and that whatever the future might hold would be little like the past. "The last 10 years I've gone up and down the earth drinking in experience, fighting and loving, seeing and hearing and testing things. . . . I'm not quite sick of seeing yet, but soon I will be— I know that. My future life will not be what it has been. And so I want to stop a minute, and look back, and get my bearings" (125).

To get his bearings, John Reed would have had to look back on a life that was quite different from his present one. He was no longer the buoyant youth who had bounded confidently into New York from Harvard seven years earlier. He was larger, a bit more fleshy, his forehead seemed even broader and the nose that had suggested the name "potato face" to Pancho Villa was more pronounced. Yet the intense brown eyes, unruly hair, and infectious smile were the same. Ambitious still, hard working, and unpredictable as ever, Reed had developed a deep contempt for middle-class values; he was no longer as concerned about social acceptance as he had once been at Harvard. His experiences in Paterson, Mexico, Ludlow, his work on the *Masses,* and his travels through war-torn Europe had also increased his consciousness of social injustice. Reed was a radical, but his beliefs had evolved more from what he had seen and experienced than from what he had read. For Reed, seeing and experiencing were always the best ways to learn. Although experience remained Reed's most constant teacher, by the time he was thirty he had sampled widely in the literature of socialism as well. Max Eastman recalled the special tutoring Reed received in Provincetown during the summer of 1915 from the English Marxist, Fred Boyd. During that summer of theatrical experimentation, Boyd lived in the chaotic Reed household. "Fred was leading Jack's eager mind beyond *The Masses* editorials into the absolute Calvin-logic of Marxian fundamentalism," Eastman wrote years later after he had broken with the Left.[38] Thus personal experience and sporadic periods of reading had nurtured Reed's radicalism. His changing views ultimately led him to question his own privileged position in an inegalitarian society. "All I know is that my happiness is built on the misery of other people, so that I eat because others go hungry, that I am clothed when other people go almost naked through the frozen cities in winter; and that fact poisons me, disturbs my serenity" ("Almost Thirty" 142).

Despite embracing the Left, Reed was never motivated only by political concerns, nor did he ever become a deeply political person. To be sure he was aware of and sensitive to human suffering and social injustice around him. What he had seen made it impossible for him to go back to the carefree concerns of earlier years. But his innate qualities always competed with his political concerns. Reed was intensely ambitious, he wanted to be at the center of the action, he strongly believed in himself as a writer and a poet, he genuinely loved adventure, and he always tried to experience life at its fullest. As a result he lived in a rush of activity and creativity.

The fall of 1917 found Reed disillusioned and, as he claimed, saturated with "seeing." Nevertheless, he still hoped that the *Metropolitan* would send him to China to observe events there firsthand,

and in the process, to revitalize his journalistic skills. He claimed
he would gladly leave Europe and the United States behind. As he
concluded his autobiographical essay: "The whole Great War is to
me just a stoppage of the life and ferment of human evolution. I
am waiting, waiting for it all to end, for life to resume so I can
find my work" (143). Reed had no way of knowing then that he
would find his work again soon. Nor could he predict that it would
be not in the Orient, but in the turmoil of revolutionary Russia.

Chapter Two
Discovery and Commitment

Reed at first showed very little interest in the Russian Revolution. His obsession with the madness of the war in Europe and its impact on his life and career seemed more important at the time. Early on, his greatest concern was how the overthrow of the tsar and the creation of a provisional government in March 1917, would affect the war. It seemed certain that a new, liberal regime would once again strengthen the military and unite Russia against Germany. However good this might be for Russia, it would also prolong the war he hated ("Fall of the Russian Bastille," New York *Tribune,* 25 March 1917). But Reed quickly learned more about the Russian situation and when he discovered that liberals, businessmen, and army officers of the Provisional Government were not alone in the competition for power in revolutionary Petrograd, his enthusiasm grew. By early June 1917, he had heard reports that councils of workers and sailors were challenging the authority of the Provisional Government. When the *New York Times* suggested that these councils were tainted with a brand of radicalism similar to that of the IWW, Reed confidently predicted that the revolution was just beginning. "The Russian Revolution having finally shown signs of becoming actually popular, England and our best people are becoming really alarmed," he announced in an article for the *Masses* ("Too Much Democracy," June 1917). "Perhaps it was a mistake to hail 'the free Russian People'—it may be that the Council of Workingmen's and Soldiers' Delegates (who only represent the vast majority of the people) is going to have something to say" (21). Reed was soon convinced that the Russian masses were going to have considerably more to say than he had ever dreamed, and he apologized to the "Russian proletariat" for having misgauged their revolution. Now as he understood their aims, he explained to his readers: "the real thing was the long-thwarted rise of the Russian masses, as now we see with increasing plainness; and the purpose of it is the establishment of a new human society upon the earth" ("The Russian Peace," *Masses,* July 1917, 35). Predicting such a

monumental creation was one thing, but actually seeing it emerge
was something else, and Reed was soon eagerly searching for a way
to get to Russia.

Russia And Revolution

It is tempting to read backwards from Reed's later commitment
to the Russian Revolution and interpret his eagerness to go to Russia
in the summer of 1917 in purely political terms. As sympathetic
as he was with the news coming out of Russia during that exciting
spring and summer, his initial desire to get there was largely tied
to personal and professional needs. With his marriage failing and
his career in decline, he seized the chance to leave disappointments
behind and to travel to the site of revolutionary upheaval. Just as
four years earlier Mexico had been a springboard to adventure and
fame, so too he thought might revolutionary Russia. Reed could
also escape a war-aroused America with its insistence upon patriotic
conformity. Hoping that Louise, who was still in France, might
arrange to meet him, he eagerly wrote to her that July: "If I got a
chance to go to Russia via Vladivostok, could you go to Petrograd,
via Stockholm, and wait for me there? We'd come back, of course,
by China."[1] Revolutionary Russia, then, was to be experienced,
savored, and of course, written about, but so too was China, which
Reed had postponed visiting the previous fall because of his kidney
operation. As Reed's commitment to the revolution grew like hybrid
seed in virgin soil, he quickly forgot the trip to China. But in the
summer of 1917, Reed the journalist was still planning to write
about the revolution, not to join it.

It was ultimately Max Eastman who helped Reed get to Russia,
for he too was excited by reports of the revolution. It troubled him
that the one writer he thought capable of understanding the turmoil
of radical change was in New York and not in Petrograd. In the
midst of his own battle to keep the *Masses* afloat and to prevent
government censorship, Eastman found the time to raise two thousand dollars from a New York socialite to finance his friend's way.
Thus by early August, Reed's luck seemed to be on the upswing.
He and Louise were reunited. She had wrangled a commission from
the Bell syndicate to study the revolution from a woman's perspective, and they were planning a trip to Russia together.

As he sailed in mid-August 1917, on the Danish steamer the

United States, Reed closely observed the strange assortment of passengers intent on going to Russia. Each seemed to interpret the
revolution in a different light, particularly since no one seemed to
know who was in control. Traveling through Scandinavia Reed and
Louise heard rumors that General Kornilov supported by his savage
division of Cossacks was bringing down the Provisional Government
in Petrograd while battling with the city's workers.

When they reached Petrograd in early September, Jack and Louise
found that Kornilov's coup d'etat had failed. City life, oddly enough,
was reminiscent of a carnival. During the day, power and food
shortages created long lines for basic necessities while at night the
cabarets, hotels, and the opera served a seemingly insatiable clien-
tele. Political affairs were equally confusing. The Provisional Government challenged the Petrograd Soviet and the Central Committee
of Soviets for control of the city and perhaps the entire country. In
mid-July, Alexander Kerensky had become premier in a reorganized
Provisional Government. He continued to support the Russian war
effort as he tried to check the growing power of the Soviets. The
Soviets included Mensheviks, Bolsheviks, and Socialist Revolutionaries, all struggling with the Provisional Government and with each
other for supremacy. On 17 July 1917, the most militant of these
revolutionary groups, the Bolsheviks, had supported a spontaneous
but unsuccessful attempt by groups of soldiers and sailors to overthrow the Provisional Government. The Bolsheviks were then forced
to go underground. By the end of July most of their leaders were
either in jail or in exile. But less than two months later, the Bolsheviks emerged from the confusion of the Kornilov Affair as one
of the most powerful parties in the city. Apparently misinterpreting
the intentions of the Kerensky group, Kornilov, with middle-class
support, seemed ready to seize control of the government. Reacting
to the threat, Kerensky created a Military Revolutionary Committee
in which the Bolsheviks were allowed to participate. When the
Kornilov attack failed, the Bolsheviks emerged as the only winners.
Their popularity had increased in the wake of their militant defense
of the revolution, and by arming the workers they controlled the
largest, most dependable military force in Petrograd.

Arriving in the midst of this turmoil in early September, Reed
and Bryant found a room at the same hotel where John and Boardman
Robinson had stayed a year earlier while covering the war in Eastern
Europe. Seeing the hotel staff once again reminded Reed of past

escapades, but the atmosphere in Petrograd was so different that he tried to describe the changes to his former traveling companion. "The old town has changed! Joy where there was gloom, and gloom where there was joy. We are in the middle of things, and believe me it's thrilling."[2] Yet being in the "middle of things" could also be confusing. Reed better understood the constantly fluctuating political situation when he met a former acquaintance, Albert Rhys Williams, who was reporting on the revolution for the *New York Post*. Trained in the ministry, Williams had gravitated towards social reform. By the time they met in Petrograd, he and Reed were temperamentally much alike. Eager to catch up on all that he had missed, Reed frantically questioned Williams about the position of the Provisional Government, the composition of the Soviets, and especially about the personalities of such Bolshevik leaders as Lenin and Trotsky. As Williams, Reed, and Bryant roamed the city's streets trying to anticipate the most vital points of activity, they were often joined by Bessie Beatty of the San Francisco *Bulletin*. Several Russian-Americans who had become committed Bolsheviks when they returned to Russia in 1917 helped the four correspondents untangle the political situation and the Russian language as well. Williams later admitted that this kind of help must have biased their views of the revolution, but the Russian-Americans enabled him and Reed to gather information in a country whose language they scarcely understood.[3]

Despite the language barrier, Reed and Williams could sense that the Provisional Government lacked the support of the city's working classes. As they left the Duma one day, tired of listening to speeches, they encountered a worker who seemed equally bored. In faltering Russian they tried to question him about his views of the political situation and whether or not he supported the Provisional Government. "The worker looked again at these two strange young men, spat out a sunflower seed or two, shook his head, and said slowly," according to Williams years later, " 'I don't know why you ask. This is not my government. This may be *your* war, but it's not mine. You are bourgeois and I am a worker.' "[4] Such a rebuff might have offended other correspondents, but it was the kind of statement that would have excited Reed. Here were workers unlike those in Europe and America. Russians would not be led off to the trenches for lofty principles or nationalistic justifications that did not touch their lives. They depended on no one but themselves. In contrast,

Reed recalled his own fumbling efforts to aid American workers. "What counts is what we do when we go home," he remarked one day to Williams. "It's easy to be fired by things here. We'll wind up thinking we're great revolutionaries. And at home? . . . Oh, I can always put on another pageant!"[5]

Such introspective brooding was a luxury for Reed. Usually he and his fellow reporters were rushing about the city observing the growing power of the Bolsheviks and the faltering efforts of the Provisional Government. A trip with Williams to the Russian army along the Latvian front brought home to Reed how unpopular the war was among the common soldiers ("A Visit to the Army—II," *Liberator,* May 1918). Later in the month he and Louise arranged an interview with Kerensky. The head of the Provisional Government received them in the tsar's private library, and reminded the two Americans that the French Revolution had taken five years and that the Russian Revolution was just beginning ("Red Russia—Kerensky," *Liberator,* April 1918, 18). Soon after his meeting with Kerensky, Reed visited an arms factory in the Viborg sector of the city. When he told an audience of workers and sailors that he brought them greetings from American workers, a soldier asked him to deliver a message: "I ask American comrades to carry back word to America that Russians will never give up their revolution until they are killed. That they will hold the fort with all their strength until the peoples of world rise and help them."[6] By the end of October, Reed had seen enough to convince him that the Bolsheviks were the only party in Russia who understood the demands of the masses. Sharing his feelings once again with his former traveling companion Boardman Robinson, he wrote: "What do the masses of the Russian people want? First, peace then land; then a true democratic republic—and for the present time, before the Constituent Assembly, all the power to go to the Soviets of Workmen, Soldiers, and Peasants, that spontaneous proletarian government born of the revolution." What he added next was something that he had begun to feel in Paterson, and then more strongly in Mexico and Ludlow, but had been unable to articulate until he spent six weeks in revolutionary Russia. "I have so far learned one lesson, I think; and that is that as long as this world exists, the 'working class and the capitalist class have nothing in common.' "[7]

By the end of October 1917, Reed and his fellow Americans knew one of the worst kept secrets in all of Petrograd—that the Bolsheviks were planning an armed uprising very soon. He and his friends haunted Bolshevik headquarters at Smolny Institute, the former girl's boarding school in the eastern part of the city, hoping to be present when the rumored seizure of power occurred. On 30 October, Jack learned from Leon Trotsky that the Provisional Government was powerless and could no longer guide the revolution.[8] Despite the expected storm, Petrograd remained outwardly calm. When the Bolshevik coup eventually came, it was almost anticlimactic. The Provisional Government seemed to disappear as much from exhaustion as from inertia.

John and Louise were close enough to the center of activity to see many of the events that led to the fall of the old order. After seeing a movie on the night of 6 November, they returned to Smolny to learn that the important Peter-Paul Fortress across the Neva from the Winter Palace was under Soviet control. Several hours later as they were leaving Smolny, an excited Russian-American friend and former IWW member, Bill Shatov, rushed up to Reed shouting: "We're off! Kerensky sent the *yunkers* to close down our papers, *Soldat* and *Rabotchi Put*. But our troops went down and smashed the Government seals, and now we're sending detachments to seize the bourgeois newspaper offices!" (*Ten Days* 62).

For the next few days Reed experienced both weariness and excitement. At first, he, Bryant, and Williams wandered throughout the city trying to find visible signs of change. When they found the Winter Palace surrounded by soldiers of unknown loyalties, they were able to get through by flashing their American press cards. Once inside they learned that Kerensky had left the city for the front. They also noticed that the inside of the palace looked less like a seat of government than the barracks of a demoralized army. Mattresses, blankets, cigarette butts, and groups of confused and frightened soliders were everywhere. A Bolshevik attack was expected at any moment. Reed and his friends left the Winter Palace and walked through the still bustling city. Instead of attending the ballet that night as they had planned, they went to Smolny to see the meeting of the Second Congress of Soviets. The session lasted well into the early hours of the next morning. As the Bolsheviks won a majority of seats on the Soviet's presidium, the sound of artillery fire reminded the congress that the struggle for Petrograd continued. Around four that morning Reed, Bryant, Williams, Beatty, and a Russian-American, Alex Gomberg, stumbled out of

Smolny into the cold air to find a truck being loaded with bundles of proclamations. Told that they could go along, the Americans climbed in. They were soon jolting along city streets leaving the blazing lights of Smolny far behind. "One man tore the wrapping from a bundle and began to hurl handfuls of paper into the air," Reed later remembered. "We imitated him, plunging down through the dark street with a tail of white papers floating and eddying out behind. The late passerby stopped to pick them up; the patrols around bonfires on the corners ran out with uplifted arms to catch them. Sometimes armed men loomed up ahead, crying 'Shtoi!' and raising their guns, but our chauffeur only yelled something unintelligible and we hurtled on" (*Ten Days* 95). The leaflets proclaimed the overthrow of the Provisional Government, although Reed's throwing them from the truck reflected little more than his own excitement. But this spontaneous act also revealed his growing sense of commitment to the revolution, a commitment that deepened during the weeks ahead.

The leaflets Reed had strewn about the city announced what was not yet entirely true, for when the truck arrived at the Winter Palace, the building was still in the hands of the Provisional Government. With little time to spare, Reed and his friends joined a crowd of thousands as it rushed towards that great lighted structure and overpowered the Provisional Government. For the second time in a day, Reed wandered through the corridors of the Winter Palace. This time he saw soldiers and sailors challenging looters. Reed watched as soldiers marched out remnants of the Provisional Government to the Peter-Paul Fortress. He then returned briefly to the Smolny Institute to celebrate with the victors. At 6:00 A.M. Jack and Louise finally staggered back to their hotel, exhausted but exhilarated.

Jack's victory excitement was premature. Even though the Provisional Government had fallen, the Bolshevik Revolution was by no means secure. Over the next few days Reed watched the continuing struggle for power rage throughout the city. He saw Lenin for the first time on 8 November, as he addressed the second session of the Congress of Soviets. When the congress rose and sang the "International" and the "Funeral March" for those who had died in the war, John and Louise marveled at the solidarity of the moment. Two days later, Reed and Williams visited the outskirts of the city to watch a motley army of soldiers and workers prepare to repel

attacks by counterrevolutionary forces. With the Bolsheviks consolidating their power in Petrograd, Jack and Louise's interest shifted
to Moscow. There it was rumored that in seizing the city the Bolsheviks had severely damaged the Kremlin. Reed and Bryant left
for Moscow on 20 November, eager to view the progress of the
revolution in another setting. They found that the fighting in Moscow had been more intense than in Petrograd, but that the Kremlin
had escaped with only minor damage. They also saw the preparation
of a mass grave beside the Kremlin walls to honor the five hundred
workers and soldiers who had died while fighting for control of the
city. On the day of the funeral, Louise and Jack stood for hours in
bitterly cold weather to watch the endless lines of Russian people
who had come to honor these revolutionary heroes. It was a scene
that Reed could not forget: "I suddenly realized that the devout
Russian people no longer needed priests to pray them into heaven.
On earth they were building a kingdom more bright than any heaven
had to offer, and for which it was a glory to die" (Ten Days 259).
Ironically, a little less than two years later Reed would join these
fallen heroes of the revolution beneath the Kremlin walls. But in
the fall of 1917, he was full of life and no longer content to stand
on the sidelines while others erected the new Secular Kingdom. He
wished to help build it himself.

Shortly after he returned from Moscow, Reed and his friend
Williams joined the newly organized Bureau of International Revolutionary Propaganda. The bureau was a part of the Ministry of
Foreign Affairs under the direction of Karl Radek and was intended
to solidify the revolution in Russia by spreading its principles into
neighboring countries. Reed and Williams worked under the direct
supervision of Boris Reinstein. He had gone to Europe as a member
of the American Socialist Labor party to attend a socialist convention
in Sweden, but had converted to Bolshevism and wound up in
Russia. Under Reinstein's guidance, the two American's primary
responsibility was to glorify revolutionary ideals in pamphlets, leaflets, newspapers, and any other kind of material that could be
distributed to German and Austrian troops or prisoners of war.
Williams and Reed brought modern advertising techniques to the
bureau in the brief, concrete images they used.[9]

During the rest of his stay in Russia, Reed divided his time
between journalism, earning money, and increasing his involvement
in the revolution. Economic need was his most immediate concern.

He had already spent most of the money he had brought, and the salary he earned from his work for the Bureau of Propaganda was not enough to cover expenses. Money problems led Reed to help Colonel Raymond Robins of the American Red Cross start an American newspaper in Petrograd. Unlike most American officials then in Russia, Robins accepted the Bolsheviks, but he shared with his compatriots an overwhelming concern for keeping them in the war. Robins believed that a normalization of relations between the United States and the Bolsheviks was one way of insuring Russian wartime commitment. He was convinced that trade was the magnet that would hold the two countries together. An English-language newspaper could outline potential investment opportunities for both sides. Robins turned to Reed for technical advice. Reed was eager to earn some money, but wary of the project's capitalist underpinnings. He agreed to help so long as he would not be associated with the finished product. Rationalizing his role in setting up the paper, he explained to Williams: "I dummied in a line under the masthead: 'This paper is devoted to promoting the interests of American capital!' "[10] Despite Reed's efforts to disassociate himself as far as possible from the newspaper, his activities on its behalf would return to haunt him a few weeks later.

In the beginning of the new year, Reed received disturbing news from home. The government had suspended publication of the *Masses* and had indicted him and the other editors for conspiracy. Even before this news arrived, he and Louise had been planning to return home, but they postponed their departure until after the meeting of the Constituent Assembly in mid-January 1918. The Bolsheviks had planned the assembly months before. At that time they exploited the failure of the Kerensky government by calling elections and arousing opposition across the country. Now in control, they held elections and the assembly gathered, although it was never meant to play an important role.

Reed attended the first and only session of the Constituent Assembly on 18 January. When the Bolsheviks quickly dissolved the assembly for being counterrevolutionary, Reed was not concerned. He believed that it no longer represented the interests of either the masses or the revolution. For him the high point of the session was his introduction to Lenin. Expecting to hear Lenin's analysis of the political situation, Reed instead received a friendly lecture on the systematic approach that he would have to adopt to learn Russian.[11]

On 19 January, the day the Constituent Assembly was dissolved, Reed showed both his enthusiastic support for the revolution and his disdain for American diplomats in the city. Armed with a rifle, he joined the Red Guard patrolling in front of the Foreign Affairs office. Troops had been placed there as a precaution against counterrevolutionary forces who opposed the dismissal of the Constituent Assembly. Reed may have intended to show his support of the Russian workers, but his friend, Williams, thought otherwise. Williams believed that Reed patrolled with the Red Guard to discredit the American embassy. His relations with the embassy's personnel and especially with its conservative ambassador, David R. Francis, had never been good. Reed had angered Francis by participating in a public protest against the imprisonment in America of Emma Goldman and Alexander Berkman.[12] His other activities on behalf of the Bolsheviks, including his work with the Bureau of Propaganda, made it clear where his sympathies lay. In Petrograd, Reed noticed that he was occasionally followed and he assumed that the embassy was responsible. He was not concerned until Louise was followed too. Then, according to Williams, he decided to do something that would rankle American officialdom.[13] Reed succeeded, for a few days later Edgar Sisson, a member of George Creel's Committee on Public Information, who was sent to Russia to encourage the war effort, lectured Reed on his "unacceptable" behavior. Reminding him of his background and Harvard connections, Sisson gratuitously explained that the Bolsheviks were only using him for propaganda. Reed ignored the advice. He appeared with Williams and Reinstein at the opening session of the Third Congress of Soviets on 23 January. In his greeting to the congress, Reed promised to tell American workers about everything he had seen in Russia in the hope that they too would be motivated to act.[14]

By the end of January 1918, Louise had already left for home. John was getting ready to go. His most urgent task was to secure the piles of material—posters, proclamations, and personal notes— that he had accumulated for the book he wished to write on the revolution. Fearful that these invaluable documents might be seized, he approached Trotsky about being given diplomatic immunity. To his delight, Trotsky offered to appoint him Soviet consul to New York City. Reed's biographer, Robert Rosenstone, suggests that Trotsky's offer may not have been entirely serious, but Reed treated it as though it were and was pleased with the opportunities it promised.[15] Even when a fellow journalist warned him that acceptance of the offer might result in his arrest, Reed replied: "Perhaps it is time someone went to jail. It may be the best thing I can do to advance the cause." He then lightheartedly added: "When I am consul, I suppose I shall have to marry people. I hate the marriage ceremony. I shall simply say to them: 'Proletariat of the world unite.' "[16]

Officials at the American embassy had no intention of allowing Reed to accept the consulship. Such an appointment would seriously embarrass the United States. Ambassador Francis turned to Reed's former employer, Raymond Robins, for help. Robins turned to a Russian-American, Alexander Gomberg, who had friends in the American community and the Bolshevik government. Gomberg and Reed had met when the Reeds first arrived in Petrograd, but their conflicting personalities had led to a mutual dislike. In an effort to discredit Reed, Gomberg got a copy of Reed's prospectus for an English-language newspaper, and this document eventually reached Lenin. During the later, more relaxed atmosphere of the New Economic Policy, Reed's connection with a capitalist undertaking might well have been tolerated. But times were different then, the revolution was still under attack, and the Bolsheviks withdrew Reed's appointment. He returned to the United States as a private citizen. The trip home was most unpleasant as Edgar Sisson, still galled by Reed's attitude, used his official connections to disrupt the journey.[17] Leaving Petrograd on 23 February 1918, Reed arrived in Christiania, Norway, only to discover that the State Department would not allow him to go on to the United States or return to Russia. For the next six weeks he was stranded in Norway selling articles to local newspapers to earn some money, working on a long poem about his native country, sketching out chapters for a book on the revolution, and anxiously awaiting a reunion with Louise. It was not until April that he was allowed to leave, and it was almost May when he finally reached the United States. Despite the prolonged journey home, Reed was as enchanted as ever by the Russian Revolution. Unfortunately, he came home to an America more intolerant of dissenters than it had been eight months earlier.

Wartime America

Before Reed had left for Russia the government had passed an Espionage Act that dictated severe penalties for obstructing the war effort. Shortly after his return to the United States, Congress passed a Sedition Act, which made it virtually impossible to criticize the war without reprisal. Reed learned in Petrograd that he, Max Eastman, and several other staff members of the *Masses* had been indicted under the Espionage Act for publishing material that hindered the draft. The first *Masses* trial took place while John was en route from Christiania, and ended with a hung jury the day before he arrived in New York. But Reed did not escape the country's growing paranoia. Customs officials seized his materials on the revolution and quizzed him for several hours about his activities over the preceding eight months. Only then did they allow him to keep the long-awaited reunion with Louise. But Reed's experience at customs was only a hint of things to come, for over the next few months, like a zealot among the unconverted, he faced the hazards of preaching revolutionary doctrines in an increasingly conservative atmosphere.

While Reed immediately set out to recover his confiscated papers, his most urgent problem was to earn a living. Mistrustful of his radical views, none of the commercial periodicals or newspapers would touch his articles. Louise had some success in publishing her views on the revolution, which provided them with a meager income. Reed sent virtually all his articles to the one periodical he thought might publish his work—the *Liberator*. A sequel to the *Masses,* which had ceased publication under government pressure in the fall of 1917, the *Liberator* was created by Max Eastman under the private control of Eastman and his sister, Crystal. Eastman welcomed Reed's contributions, but he also wanted the new magazine to survive and tempered its views accordingly.[18]

Unable to earn a living writing, Reed began to lecture about Russia. Over the next few months, he addressed largely working-class audiences in cities throughout the East and Midwest. Although the groups he spoke to were usually receptive to his enthusiastic greeting of "Tovarischi," and his descriptions of how worker-controlled soviets functioned, not so the local authorities who hounded his every move. In June, the Philadelphia police arrested him for breaking a local ordinance while speaking out-of-doors. Several days later police randomly arrested members of an audience he spoke to in Detroit as they left the lecture hall.[19] Undeterred, Reed went to Chicago in July to attend the trial of 113 members of the IWW who, individually, were charged with over one hundred crimes relating to sabotage, sedition, and subversion.[20] Although the Wobblies were accused of disrupting the war, from Reed's perspective they were simply fighting for what was rightfully theirs.

Despite their busy lecture schedules and frantic efforts to earn money, John and Louise found time during the summer of 1918 to be together at their cottage at Croton, some thirty miles from New York City. They had bought the cottage in 1916, and over the years it had become a refuge from the demands of their frenetic lives. While resting there, they both continued to write. In an article published in the *Liberator* in July, Reed complained bitterly that "at the present moment, however, most of the Allied Governments seem to be acting on the theory that it is more important to defeat the Russian Soviets than to defeat Germany" ("Recognize Russia," July 1918, 20).

By mid-summer 1918, Reed had been back in the United States for almost three months. He was greatly frustrated by his experiences with local police, by the government's refusal to return his papers, and by his feeling that the Wobblies were being forced into prison. The repressive atmosphere at home contrasted strongly with the exhilirating one he had left behind in Russia. Reed's anger and frustration led him to resign in August from the editorial staff of the *Liberator*. Eastman's cautious editorial policies had been bad enough, but his old friend was by then supporting the war aims of Woodrow Wilson. Reluctantly, Reed sent Eastman a letter asking that his name be removed from the editorial page, but promising that he would continue to contribute to the magazine. "The reason is," he tried to explain, "I cannot in these times bring myself to share editorial responsibility for a magazine which exists upon the sufferance of Mr. Burleson [Postmaster General]."[21]

Reed often argued his new beliefs so intensely that his friends feared he had undergone a personality change since his return from Russia. Max Eastman found that new seriousness had replaced Reed's old exuberance. "It seemed to me that a person who had seen the victory of the working classes ought to have the joy in his eyes. Instead Jack came home in a state of tension that was almost somber."[22] What Reed felt so strongly at this time was the need to defend publicly the principles of the revolution during its darkest hours.

By early September, the anti-Bolshevik forces in Russia were gaining momentum. To make matters worse, other nations, including the United States, were aiding the counterrevolution. Reed's disenchantment with his own country, especially, as he saw it, the hypocrisy of the president, spilled over in a speech at Hunt's Point Palace in New York on 14 September 1918. Two thousand people— among them agents and stenographers for the Justice Department— heard him lash out at the presence of American and Japanese troops in Russia. Predictably, Reed was arrested the next day for sedition.[23] On the same day, the national press began to carry a series of documents reputedly showing that the German government was paying key Bolshevik leaders to disrupt the Allied war effort. Forgetting his own problems, Reed quickly wrote and printed a pamphlet in which he argued that the documents assembled by his old nemesis, Edgar Sisson, were crude forgeries and yet another example of the kinds of lies being told about the Soviet regime. Reed was quite correct. But his most pressing need was to prepare his defense in connection with the second *Masses* trial scheduled to begin towards the end of September.

Even though the first *Masses* trial ended in a hung jury, the government persisted in its attempts to obtain an indictment under the Espionage Act. In the courtroom of the second trial, a nearly carnival atmosphere prevailed. Martial music from a nearby park drifted through the open windows. Many Villagers occupied the benches in a show of support for the defendants who often joked among themselves. Despite the surface lightheartedness, the trial was a serious affair. With national patriotism at an all-time high, the defendants faced a possible prison term. Reed reflected the contrast between appearances and reality when he asked Art Young, a codefendant, as they entered the courtroom: "Well, Art, got your grip packed for Atlanta?"[24] As Max Eastman recalled, Reed described the horrors of war while his eyes focused on the ceiling over the heads of the jury. "He was very boyish and high-voiced and inept and uneasy in his clothes, but all the more likable and believable because of it. Some people, you look in their eyes and you say, 'This man is honest and kind,' and you feel that no further question need be asked. Jack had such eyes."[25] Perhaps Reed's testimony helped his cause, but is was more likely an inept prosecution and Eastman's elegant three-hour summation that led to another hung jury. The government did not try the defendants again.

There was little time for celebration. Reed was still concerned that America did not understand the Bolsheviks. He believed that the continuing American intervention in the Russian civil war was based on a misguided sense of self-interest. There would come a time, he warned in an article published in the *Liberator,* when "thousands of Americans who really believe in freedom will someday want to know why America, instead of leading the liberal world, joined with those whose faces are set against the tides of history" ("On Intervention in Russia," November 1918, 17). Yet as frustrated as Reed was during the fall of 1918, two things happened in November that brightened his mood considerably. The first was the armistice that ended the war he so detested. The second was the recovery of his papers from the State Department.

For seven months Reed had waited for his papers, worried that his vivid impressions of the revolution would fade. Now that he had them in hand, he felt a familiar tension between his commitment to revolutionary ideals and his commitment to his art. Although he had been a dervish of activity on behalf of the revolution since his return from Russia, he now did nothing but write about his experiences there. With the revolution far from over, Reed temporarily blocked out the present to reconstruct the past. For the next two months he poured over his notes and documents. Reed withdrew from friends and political commitments to complete the project that he had been planning for over a year. His seclusion finally ended in early January 1919. In a remarkably short time of intensified writing, he had recaptured the excitement and complexity of the Bolshevik seizure of power. During these two months his art had dominated his life, but with *Ten Days That Shook the World* safely in the hands of a publisher, Reed put down his pen to rejoin the revolutionary fray.

Political Activities

During the first five months of 1919, Reed continued to interpret the revolution for all those willing to listen, to help spread its organizing principles to American workers, and to denounce foreign intervention in the Russian civil war. But the atmosphere in which he worked had grown dangerously hostile. Even though the war was over, intolerance was widespread, and superpatriotism, like the ash from a volcanic eruption, continued to smother the American landscape. A senate judiciary subcommittee headed by Senator Lee

S. Overman symbolized the growing fear of radicalism. Originally created to investigate the connection between the country's liquor interests and German propaganda in 1919, the committee switched its attention to Bolshevism. It began by interviewing an array of friendly witnesses who agreed to testify about their experiences in Russia. Most of them delighted in dredging up atrocities that accompanied the Bolshevik seizure of power or in describing the horrors of life in the new Soviet state. Appalled by this anti-Bolshevik publicity, Reed, Bryant, and Albert Rhys Williams volunteered to supply the committee with a different perspective. Bryant was the first to be called on 20 February. The tone of the committee's questions and her responses were set within the first few minutes. Louise was told to affirm a belief in God before taking the required oath. Angrily she suggested that the committee was trying her for witchcraft.[26] Later, when asked her class status, she quickly answered: "Well, I am very poor, so I belong to the proletariat." Reed took the stand on 21 February. After the committee listened to his interpretation of the origins of the revolution, he was questioned about his own political views. When one senator pointedly asked if he advocated revolution for the United States, Reed immediately responded: "I have always advocated a revolution in the United States." But when the startled senator questioned if he truly meant what he said, Reed safely skirted the issue by replying: "Revolution does not necessarily mean a revolution by force. By revolution I mean a profound social change. I do not know how it is to be attained." He clarified his views even more by explaining later: "I mean, of course, that the will of the people will be done, and if it cannot be done by law, it will be done by force. It never has been done peaceably, but I do not see why it should not. I still do not see why it is not. As a matter of fact, if I am saying anything which is contrary to law, I am willing to answer for it."[27]

In spite of the bravado of Reed's testimony, the committee did not try to investigate his radical views. For that matter, by the early spring of 1919, most of the indictments against him, including the one arising from his Hunt's Point Palace speech, were dropped for a variety of reasons.[28] Freed from the worry of litigation for the first time in months, Reed could not, however, escape the biting editorializing of the *New York Times*. The paper charged that he and other "local Bolsheviki hope for the triumph of the embattled proletariat, but they also hope to be here to see it and share in the profits. No martyrdom for them."[29] Angry and a bit embarrassed at this attack on his integrity, Reed answered in a way that recalled Bryant's testimony before the Overman committee: "The business of spreading what you call 'Bolshevik propaganda' is not very lucrative, as you yourself must know. There is no money in speaking to working class audiences, or writing in working class papers, which are the only audiences and papers open to any advocacy of the truth about Soviet Russia" ("On Bolshevism, Russian and American," *Revolutionary Age,* 12 April 1919, 6).

Reed's claim of poverty was not exaggerated. Since returning to the United States, neither he nor Bryant had earned much money. It was also true that nearly everything he wrote now appeared in working-class publications. He had joined the New York Socialist party shortly after returning from Russia, and in the fall of 1918 had agreed to be a contributing editor for a Boston socialist journal, *Revolutionary Age.* When a left-wing faction within the Socialist party began to emerge in the spring of 1919, he agreed to edit its journal, the *New York Communist.* Eventually the two journals merged, but in the late summer of 1919, Reed severed his ties with both over a dispute about the formation of an American Communist party. He nevertheless continued to express his views publicly after agreeing to edit the *Voice of Labor,* a periodical created by left-wing Socialists to prepare American workers for the takeover of their industrial plants. Together with the *Liberator,* these three journals were Reed's only American outlets for publication in 1919.

Writing was an important way to bring about social change, but Reed had learned in Russia the additional need for political action. While he still admired the syndicalist orientation of the IWW, he now opposed its unwillingness to enter the political arena. "If anything were needed to demonstrate the value of political action," he had written in January, "the Russian Revolution ought to do it" ("A New Appeal," *Revolutionary Age,* 18 January 1919, 8). By the spring of 1919, he was eager to put theory into practice. Despite his activism in Russia, he actually had only come to accept an activist position gradually. Committed as he had been to spreading the principles of the revolution in Russia, Reed was too much an individual and too much a writer to allow himself to be limited by a political party or an ideology. He wanted to be a dedicated revolutionary, and sacrificed much to become one. But there was always a side of Reed that preferred the freewheeling, eclectic atmosphere of the Village to the front ranks of a revolutionary party. In short, he often found it difficult to be at once a poet and a revolutionary. As he told Max Eastman, "You know, this class struggle plays hell with your poetry!"[30] It also played hell with friendships. When he ran into Lincoln Steffens in New York one evening, he accused his former mentor of lacking the fervor needed to create a revolution in America. "Why don't you join us?" Reed pleaded. "We are trying to do what you used to talk and write about."[31] The "us" Reed referred to was the American Socialist party, then in the process of undergoing sweeping change. Out of this change eventually emerged an American Communist party.

In late January 1919, the Soviet government issued a call for the creation of a Third International. Propelled by the belief that the Russian Revolution would be followed by upheavals elsewhere, Moscow also sought to purge the Left of war supporters and opponents of an immediate proletariat seizure of power. Since few American Socialists had supported the war, the American Socialist party did not split over this issue. Most American Socialists were also enthusiastic supporters of the revolution in Russia. There were, in fact, no fundamental ideological issues dividing American Socialists in early 1919, but a tactical split soon developed over how to implement the call for immediate revolution. During the first few months of 1919, the Seattle General Strike and the creation of Workers' councils in other cities of the Pacific Northwest suggested to many on the Left that a proletarian uprising was already underway. Many radicals began to feel that the traditional leadership of the American Socialist party was not militant enough to keep alive the spirit of revolution. In June, they called for a national left-wing conference in New York to bring together all those who saw the need for immediate, radical change. In the spring elections for membership on the National Executive Committee of the American Socialist party, the left-wing factions won most of the contested seats. Their victory suggested the party would soon be reshaped in the Bolshevik mold. But the old leadership refused to relinquish control. Morris Hillquit and Victor Berger instituted a sweeping purge of those suspected of supporting the left wing. This reduced party membership by more than half. With the solidarity of the American Left now broken, it was clear that American radicals could not agree on how to transmit the revolution to their own soil.[32]

Committed as he was to revolutionizing American workers, Reed found himself entwined in the internecine struggles that dominated the Left. He was one of the best-known and respected participants at the national left-wing conference, which began in Manhattan on 21 June 1919. Rather than unifying left-wing factions within the American Socialist party, the conference led to discord. By far the most divisive issue concerned the proper Socialist party image. Reed and a majority of the English-speaking delegates wanted to try and capture the party from within before seeking to create a radical party of their own. A minority of delegates wanted to disassociate themselves from the parent party completely and form an elite party patterned on the Bolsheviks. Many of those advocating the minority position were delegates from the foreign-language federations within the Socialist party. Most of the members of the federations were either Russians or Eastern Europeans, and many spoke little or no English. Far from being inhibited by the language barrier, they believed their ethnic origins gave them a special prestige. Their kinship with the revolutionaries in Russia, they said, gave them unique insight into how Bolshevism should be spread elsewhere. Reminding the majority opposition, of which Reed was a member, that the Bolsheviks had started as a small, highly organized revolutionary elite, they wanted to relegate the American Socialist party to history's scrap heap. They certainly did not want to use it as Reed had envisioned to spread the revolution. When their tactics were rejected they left the New York gathering with plans to create an American Communist party in late August.

Such deep divisions in the American Socialist party were not ideological. At the heart of the New York dispute was a matter of timing. Should the left-wing factions form an American Communist party immediately or try, knowing that there was little chance of success, to take over the American Socialist party? Another divisive issue hinged on the question of American uniqueness. Reed and most of the other English-speaking delegates like Bertram D. Wolfe, James Larkin, and Louis Frania, believed that the new American Revolution was bound to differ considerably from its parent in Russia. Tactically they still hoped to capture the American Socialist party for revolutionary purposes, and they made plans to attend its convention on 30 August 1919.

While trying to sow the seeds of revolution in his own country, Reed was discovering how unpredictable and treacherous maneuvering on the Left could be. Towards the end of July, for example, he learned that Wolfe and Frania, who had supported the majority position at the New York conference, now decided to join with the foreign-language federations to form a Communist party as quickly as possible. Despite this setback, he still hoped to capture the Socialist party from within. Reed and his fellow radicals dutifully showed up at the opening session of the Chicago convention of the American Socialist party on the morning of 30 August. But the old guard leaders of the party were ready for them. With the help of the Chicago police, Reed and his fellow delegates were expelled from the convention floor. Undaunted, he and some eighty-two other delegates gathered elsewhere in the same building and formed the Communist Labor party, a body distinct from the Communist party of the foreign-language federations, which was formed a few days later. Art Young, a friend of Reed's, remembered that Reed "was in the most playful and yet the most serious mood in which I had ever seen him. When his group opened their convention they sang the *Internationale* with a gusto which resounded throughout the building and into the street."[33] Yet revolutionary enthusiasm could not mask the fact that when Reed's group failed to gain control of the American Socialist party, there was no longer any fundamental issue dividing the two factions. More important, there was also no need for two Communist parties in America. But the bitterness lingered. And the whole episode hinted at the internal conflict that would continue to hinder the birth of communism in America.

In early September 1919, there were halfhearted attempts at reconciliation, but the Communist party, which now had the larger total membership, proclaimed itself the dominant organization. Reed found himself in opposition to those who believed that what would work in Russia would work at home. Each party took special delight in denouncing the heretical views of the other while swearing complete allegiance to the Communist International. With little hope for compromise, it was obvious that the conflict would have to be settled by the new pontiffs of the Communist world in Moscow. Because of his previous trip to Russia and his familiarity with many of the original Bolsheviks, Reed was the logical agent of the Communist Labor party. By mid-September, he was preparing to go to Russia once again. One of his most difficult tasks was to convince Louise that the trip was necessary and would be short. There was also the problem of how to get to Russia since his radical activities made him a persona non grata with the State Department. One evening in late September, he disguised himself as a sailor and with forged papers, boarded a Scandinavian freighter. Reed was going to work his way across the Atlantic just as he had nine years earlier after graduating from Harvard. But this time he was no carefree student, searching for adventure. Instead, Reed represented the revolutionary organization that hoped to become the acknowledged Communist party in America. As he jauntily walked up the gangplank and waved goodby to Louise, he had no way of knowing that he would never come home again.

In Russia Again

Reed's efforts to reach Russia were difficult but exciting. The excitement was less attractive for him now—he was a radical on a mission, not a journalist in search of copy. He jumped ship in Bergen and with the help of leftist sympathizers made his way across Norway to Christiania where he wrote to Louise of his safe arrival. "It is much worse in these countries now than it was a little while ago," he informed her. "The police have been very active, and have caught a lot of couriers and broken up the organization. But I have a fine chance to get through, and once in Stockholm, there will soon be an attempt to get to Russia."[34] After reaching Stockholm, he went by ship across the Baltic into Finland. Reed arrived in the Finnish port of Abo towards the end of October. There he experienced delays and close calls. He described his frustrations in a letter to Louise, written in early November. "I stowed away in a ship to Abo, and from there got across the country by devious ways to this place, from which I expected to start eastward any minute. . . . But of course things began to happen at once. Suddenly there were terrible police raids at Viborg."[35] Finally, by the middle of the month, he was able to travel overland to the country he had been trying to reach for six weeks.

As Jack made his way towards the new capital in Moscow, he encountered a Russia different from the one he had known. Civil war and foreign intervention continued to devastate the country. Everywhere he saw famine, typhus, and little fuel for the bitter winter. Moved by the suffering, he rejected comfortable living quarters and a meal ticket available to important visitors for a room in a working-class neighborhood where he could prepare his own food.[36] He then presented his report on the differences between the two

American Communist factions to the Executive Committee of the
Communist International. While awaiting the committee's reply,
he explored the country.

During his travels over the next two months, Reed learned how
truly disruptive radical social upheaval could be. Yet he also found
most of the workers as determined as ever to see the revolution
through the bad times. In Serpukhov, a textile city to the south of
Moscow, a worker told Reed of all the hardships that they had
endured, but then added: "Never shall the Russian workers give up
their Revolution. We die for Socialism, which perhaps we shall
never see" ("Soviet Russia Now—I," *Liberator*, December 1920,
10).

By mid-January 1920, Jack was once again making plans to return
home. The executive committee of the Communist International
had reached a decision, and, not surprisingly, had demanded the
unification of the two American factions. At this point Reed might
well have felt discouraged. He had seen tremendous suffering in
Russia. The Comintern's decision was no victory. Moreover, he was
returning home to a truly repressive atmosphere reflected by the
Palmer raids and his own indictment for radicalism. Yet the continuation of the revolution revived him. Reed spent many hours in
Moscow arguing with Emma Goldman, the deported American
anarchist, about the current status of the revolution. Goldman later
recalled that Reed also expressed concern for his own safety since
he would have to travel through counterrevolutionary countries bor-
dering the Soviet Union.[37] His concerns were more than justified.
Twice he tried to leave Russia and twice he was forced to turn back.
Finally, in mid-March a third attempt through Finland ended in
disaster. The Finnish police found him hiding in the engine room
of a freighter docked in Abo and arrested him. Reed was carrying
jewels and currency provided by the Soviet government for the
American Communist party as well as false identity papers and other
documents that tied him to the Bolsheviks. Although officially
charged with smuggling, Reed knew the Finns were cracking down
on all leftist activities and he expected political charges as well.
While confined in a Finnish jail for weeks, he managed to leak to
the press a story of his own execution in the hope that the American
State Department would acknowledge his situation.[38] In April, he
was convicted of smuggling. Kept in solitary confinement and fed
on a monotonous diet of bread and salted fish, Reed suffered terribly.

On 3 May 1920, after eight weeks in a tiny cell, he wrote to Louise. "This case has been tried, the diamonds all confiscated, and I have been fined 5000 marks (about $250–300). . . . But this is not what keeps me in prison. It is the question of whether I have committed treason toward the Finnish state."[39] Little had changed by the middle of the month, except, as Jack again wrote to Louise, life in jail was making him "more and more nervous."[40] By the beginning of June, a desperate tone marked his correspondence. "I can only sleep about 5 hours, and so am awake, perched in a little cage, for 19 hrs. a day. This is my thirteenth week."[41] Soon after he wrote this letter, Reed was released. Since the State Department still denied him a passport, he could not yet return home. There was nowhere to go but back to Russia. When Emma Goldman found Reed at a hotel in Petrograd, she was appalled to see him with his joints swollen from malnutrition, and with an ugly rash covering his body.

For almost a month he recuperated, traveled a bit, and, like most of his fellow Muscovites, enjoyed the luxury of the all too brief Russian summer. But Reed did not relax for long. By early July he was planning to participate in the Second Congress of the Communist International, scheduled to open soon. A first congress held in March 1919, while Russia was in the midst of civil war and foreign intervention, had been very poorly attended. The purpose of the second congress was to attract radical leaders from all over the world and to send them home with thoughts of revolution. Jack cheerfully became a welcoming committee of one. He escorted delegates around the city, trying to ease any fears about the soundness of the Soviet state. He was thrilled to mingle with radicals from so many different parts of the world who shared his ideals and commitment: "German Sparticides, American I.W.W.'s, Hungarian Soviet and Red Army leaders, British Shop Stewards, and Clyde Workers' Committees, Dutch transport workers, Hindu, Korean, Chinese and Persian insurrectionists" ("The World Congress of the Communist International," *Communist,* no. 10, p. 1).

Reed was one of the best-known delegates at the Congress. He was appointed to two of the special commissions that were to report to the congress on the issue of "National Minorities and the Colonial Question," and on "Trade Union Activities." Although hailed by the Soviets as an expert on the "Negro Question," Reed had little knowledge or even interest in the issue. Instead, he addressed most of his attention to the question of trade unions. In doing so, he soon found himself in direct ideological conflict with two of the most powerful figures at the congress: Grigory Zinoviev and Karl Radek. In recognizing that worldwide revolution would not happen soon, these men sought the spread of communist doctrine in the most expedient and practical way. Reed still clung to idealism and confrontational tactics. This new, more pragmatic approach of the Soviet leadership for spreading the revolution directly affected the issue of trade unions. It had been decided that the Communists would try to control traditional unions from within rather than form dual unions of their own. Reed was horrified. With his IWW background, he thought it would be a waste of time to try to cooperate with as profound a conservative as Samuel Gompers or to hope to influence an organization as elitist as the AF of L. He was convinced that industrial unionism was the only way to attract American workers, and that the AF of L, with its carefully guarded membership, was not only out of step with the working classes but also with the fundamental ideals of communism. Reed found fault with the IWW, ridiculing their fears of the dictatorship of the proletariat as so much "Anarcho-Menshevik twaddle!" ("The I.W.W. and Bolshevism," *New York Communist,* 31 May 1919, 3). But even to suggest working with the AF of L was out of the question, for this would show the same lack of familiarity with the American situation as shown by the foreign-language federations back in Chicago.

When the congress opened, Reed requested that the trade union question be placed first on the agenda because of its importance and that English be accepted as one of the official languages. Both requests were denied. No stranger to ideological confrontation, Reed was still angered by the way Zinoviev, who headed the executive committee, and Radek, who chaired the Trade Union Commission, dealt with opposition to the official line. He was even more disturbed by their autocratic style and their unbending arrogance in making decisions on issues they knew little about.[42] Despite such opponents, Reed continued to argue his position. The trade union issue totally dominated his activities at the congress, and even when reporting on the "Negro Question" he used the opportunity to attack the AF of L by denouncing its racism. American workers wanted industrial unionism, he claimed, and blacks and whites must organize into a joint labor organization.[43] When official policy line stood, Reed resigned from the committee. Persuaded to rejoin, he still would not change his views. This was clear in an article he wrote for the official organ of the Communist Party of America. Having described the struggle that had gone on within the executive committee he wrote: "After a long and bitter fight, the Executive Committee made several amendments to their theses which, although far from satisfactory to the objecting delegates, still made it possible for Communists in America to work for revolutionary industrial unionism, and for the destruction of the reactionary American Federation of Labor" ("The World Congress of the Communist International," *Communist*, no. 10, p. 2). Reed's analysis reflected his hopes rather than any official change in policy. It also showed his willingness to oppose publicly what was considered party doctrine.

Reed remained bitter about the defeat of his views during the weeks after the congress.[44] Not yet recovered from his Finnish ordeal, his mental strain only added to his weariness. In mid-August, his mood brightened when he learned that Louise was on her way to Russia. He expected their reunion would bring a period of calm in which he could resume writing. But his personal needs had to yield to official duties. Reed received orders to attend a Congress of Oriental Nations at Baku.

The original purpose of the Baku conference was to encourage colonial revolts against imperialism. Potential revolutionaries from the East were invited to this city perched on the shores of the Caspian Sea. Desperately wanting to be in Moscow when Louise arrived, Jack asked that he be excused from attending, but he was told to go. To make the situation worse, Zinoviev and Radek were to be among his traveling companions. Despite all efforts to the contrary, by the end of August, Reed was crossing the vast Volga plains aboard an armored train on the last grand adventure of his life.

Reed's reluctance evaporated when he arrived at Baku. He was fascinated by the ethnic diversity of the conference delegates, their unfamiliar languages, and exotic customs. A photograph taken there shows Reed standing in shirt sleeves with open collar among an incredible array of revolutionaries.[45] Yet his high spirits were short-lived. Reed supported a call for revolution, but Zinoviev's demand for a holy war against the imperialistic powers seemed demagogic. The lavish setting and treatment of the delegates also led him to question how the participating Bolsheviks interpreted the revolution.[46]

Reed's political doubts were temporarily set aside when he traveled back to Moscow to meet Louise. She found him dramatically changed: "I found him older and sadder and grown strangely gentle and aesthetic. His clothes were just rags. He was so impressed with the suffering around him that he would take nothing for himself. I felt shocked and almost unable to reach the pinnacle of fervor that he had attained."[47] For a week they enjoyed a nearly idyllic time in Moscow. They walked about the city, visited with friends, and discussed plans for the future. Jack talked about a sequel to *Ten Days*, *From Kornilov to Brest-Litovsk*, and a long-postponed novel, which was to be based on his own adventurous life. Their conversations also touched on deeply personal matters. Jack suggested that they should have a child in the near future regardless of what awaited them back home. But most of all, as Louise remembered, he longed for home, and despite the charges he would face there, was eager to return as soon as possible.

Reed realized none of these dreams. A little over a week after returning from Baku, he became ill with what was first diagnosed as influenza. As his fever rose and his condition worsened, doctors diagnosed typhus. Several days later, Reed suffered a stroke that paralyzed the right side of his body. Five days later on 17 October 1920, he died. His burial befitted a Soviet hero. After a brief service in the Trades Union Hall, his coffin was transported to a site alongside the Kremlin wall. There he was buried, signifying his commitment to the revolution. Attached to the wall above his grave was a large, red banner with gold lettering proclaiming a message that would have pleased him greatly: "The leaders die, but the cause lives on."[49]

Reed's Disillusionment

Reed's unexpected death raises questions about how he saw the revolution at the time. Did he still support it, or was his own disillusionment with communism leading him to break with the movement he had so faithfully served? Several friends and acquaintances who saw him during this last period in Russia were convinced that his disenchantment was profound. The fact that they saw him shortly before he died lends credibility to their views. Yet it must be remembered that such friends as Emma Goldman, who often contradicted herself, Angelica Balabanoff and Marguerite Harrison were all extremely dissatisfied with the Soviet regime and may have projected onto Reed much of their own discontent. They may also have misinterpreted his dislike of individuals or events and read into this criticism their own dislike of where the revolution was going.[50] Louise Bryant was in the best position to determine Reed's mood at the time of his death, but she died with the issue unresolved. Although she wrote that Jack was eager to return home, she never mentioned his disillusionment in any of her later writing.[51] There is little doubt that Reed intensely disliked Zinoviev and Radek and deeply mistrusted their maneuverings. There is also little doubt that he continued to oppose the party's stand on the trade union issue and was determined to continue his opposition. Rosenstone, Reed's most recent and thorough biographer, argues convincingly that while it is difficult to imagine Reed defending or even fitting into the narrow channels of Stalinism, he had invested far too much of himself in the revolution to have easily abandoned it.[52] Without convincing evidence, perhaps the best way to analyze Reed's revolutionary views at the time of his death is to do so by looking at the total man. His friend and companion, Albert Rhys Williams, took such an approach: "Even now, I cannot look at the photographs of Reed taken in that Finnish prison where he lived on frozen fish for more than two months without wanting to fight his traducers. I look at that face, gaunt and defiant, and feel anger at all those who have tried to show Reed as disillusioned when he died. I was not there, nor were they, but Louise Bryant was—and it was only after her death that the legend of the disillusioned Reed was blown up by those who were themselves disillusioned."[53] Written almost half a century after Reed's death, Williams' analysis has a ring of authenticity. Reed was far too committed to the ideals of the revolution to have turned so quickly from them. It was as a Communist—an American Communist—that he was buried beside the Kremlin wall.

Chapter Three
Development of a Writer

During the exciting days of the October Revolution, Reed met a young writer and party member, Elizabeth Drabkina, with whom he became friends. Since both shared a commitment to the revolution and to their profession, the friendship continued even when they were apart and when Reed returned to Russia in the fall of 1918. Many years later Drabkina recalled his Spartan life-style and the drab simplicity of his little room in a working-class district in Moscow. "It was here, in this room, that Reed often told us about what he had seen and experienced," she later wrote. "We felt towards him the way we felt towards all our comrades: he was the same kind of communist as we all were, except that he was an American." She also remembered his enthusiasm for his writing, especially a projected book that was to examine the revolution after the Bolshevik seizure of power. "His attitude towards this book was such that he wanted to write it in capital letters," Drabkina wrote. But it was not just Reed's interest in writing that so impressed her, it was also his willingness to use writing as a vehicle for implementing change. While proclaiming his intentions to begin work on a sequel to *Ten Days That Shook the World,* he stated emphatically that "an artillery shell, a peal of thunder, or the ocean surf does not possess the power of the book that is lying on the desk."[1] Drabkina's memories may well have been influenced by the literary constraints of socialist realism, but they are certainly correct on one point. Shortly before his death, Reed was still eager to serve the revolution, believing that he could do so most effectively with his pen.

Writing was still very much on Reed's mind several months later while he and Louise were enjoying their brief reunion after his return from the Baku conference. In a letter to Reed's mother, Louise described their last days together. "We spoke often of home and of you and we thought how we could see you when we came back— and we talked of long vacations when Jack could finish his history. He had a novel all planned out and many stories."[2] Even as death approached, Reed never lost his enthusiasm for writing. And he would write not just for the revolution, but also for the sheer joy of writing creatively. Ironically, Reed is best remembered for his adventures around the world, his many love affairs, his pranks, his sense of humor, and his commitment to revolution. Yet the one constant in this often frantic and tragically shortened life was an unwavering desire to write and to write well. While the myths about Reed live on, his writing deserves the same close scrutiny that is usually paid to his life and activities.

Early Efforts

From an early age Reed enjoyed writing, although there is little evidence of just how much he wrote as a child. In "Almost Thirty," he claims that at age nine he had already decided on writing as a career and had started a comic history of the United States patterned on the exaggerated humor of lecturer and writer Bill Nye. Later he devoted his creative energies to writing and directing the plays that he and his brother produced for their parents. The only survivor of these early creative efforts is a short essay written at age sixteen describing a camping trip on the Willamette River. Except for demonstrating a flare for the dramatic, relatively well-developed descriptive abilities, and a youthful inclination to romanticize the mundane, "The Best Camping Experience" suggests that he was still a writer more in ambition than in fact.[3]

During the years that Reed spent at Portland Academy and Morristown, he was not as self-consciously devoted to writing as many other young, would-be authors of roughly the same period. Malcolm Cowley, for example, twelve years Reed's junior, provides an interesting contrast. Recalling his high school years in *Exile's Return,* Cowley describes how the commitment that he and several of his friends felt towards writing careers separated them from most of their fellow classmates. "We felt that we were different from other boys: we admired and hated these happy ones, these people competent for every situation, who drove their fathers' cars and led the cheers at football games and never wrote poems or questioned themselves."[4] Lonely during much of his youth and fearing his own inadequacy, Reed may well have shared many of these same feelings. But by the time he reached prep school he wanted to be at the center of practically every schoolboy activity. In this respect he appears to have viewed writing not only as something he enjoyed doing, but also as a vehicle for acceptance and recognition. This need for peer recognition also helps to explain why he was so eager to display his writing skills in as many different ways and publications as possible. At Morristown, for example, writing stories and poems for the school literary magazine was simply not enough; this is why he undertook editing and doing most of the writing for what was intended as a humorous publication, the *Rooster*. In short, his early efforts at writing were yet another means by which he tried to control his environment and become one of the fellows. He did not experience the self-conscious commitment to an art that, in Cowley's case, divided him from his classmates.

A sampling of his writing at Morristown suggests that these early literary efforts were remarkably ordinary. The technique and form of his poetry was conventional and was thematically tied to the English authors or historical events that he was studying at the time. In one of his best early poems, "Lines to Tennyson," he pleads for an inspiration similar to that which had inspired the poet laureate:

> Singer of the kingly Arthur
> Deathless song which cannot die.
> To thy truth I'd fall a martyr,
> Truth from lips that will not lie.
>
> Give to me thine inspiration,
> Let thy soul my soul immerse
> Till through sweetest mediation
> I can sing my soul in verse.[5]

A less successful effort was "Sonnet to a Daisy" (*Morristonian*, June 1906), in which he apologized to Milton while trying to parody "To the Nightingale":

> Oh Daisy, thee I envy, to be sure,
> Who dost not have to do a stroke of work.
> No damages in thy existence lurk.
> Thou art from indigestion secure
> And yet thy collar clean will always be,
> Thy hands and face washed automatically,
> And lastly thou wilt peacefully lie low
> Within the bosky shades of some dun cow.

In "Lost," on the other hand, he joins with Tennyson in lamenting the passing of Arthur, and, with all of the world-weariness of a nineteen-year-old, romanticizes the past at the expense of the present:

> The old true days are gone, the future lies
> As dark and cheerless as the morning grey
> A dreary life before my saddened eyes
> Unfolds, as wearily I go my way
> While in my heart, from out the darkness rise
> The happy memories of yesterday.[6]

In view of his later career, Reed's early prose is more interesting as an example of his development as a writer, although it is as predictably romantic and imitative as his poetry. An early short story, "A Typical Yankee Tale" (*Morristonian*, November 1904), which he wrote during his first year at prep school, was undoubtedly influenced by Mark Twain's *Connecticut Yankee in King Arthur's Court.* Mixing elements of the tall tale with realistic descriptions, the story describes the adventures of a shipwrecked salesman of fireworks who uses his wares to become chief medicine man to a South American Indian tribe. Eventually the salesman has to flee for his life when the tribe's real medicine man tampers with his fireworks, thereby destroying the salesman's magical powers. A year later Jack wrote "The Transformation" (*Morristonian*, January 1905), the only one of his stories that in any way dealt with his prep school environment. The hero in the story is knocked unconscious while scoring the winning touchdown in the school's big game, and awakens as an Indian brave whose tribe is engaged in a life-and-death struggle with a neighboring tribe. When the chief, who is also the young brave's father, laments the loss of many warriors who have been killed while trying to discover the secret hiding place of their enemy, the hero volunteers for the perilous mission. He too is captured, and as the enemy hatchet crashes down on his skull he awakens in his dormitory room to the strains of the school song and to his classmates' cheers for his game-winning play. At times Reed attempted in his stories little more than vivid description, and "The End of the World" (*Morristonian*, December 1905) is a wooden, plotless sketch in which cataclysmic destruction follows a prophecy of doom. Yet on occasion Jack could display an imaginative cleverness. "The Tragedy of a Well-Mannered Man" (*Morristonian*, Jan-

uary 1906), written during his last year at Morristown, is filled
with the extravagant kind of humor that characterized much of his
writing at Harvard. The story outlines the misadventures of a man
sent by his wife to make a purchase at a department store. Unnerved
by the combativeness of bargain day, he forgets his instructions and
madly engages in a frenzy of useless buying encouraged by an army
of obliging clerks. "I lost my home, my position, my appointment,
my mind, and everything but this infernal cargo," concludes the
tormented husband. "Behold in me the awful example of an obliging
man. A department store is worse than a battle" (5).

Most of the writing Reed did at prep school is imitative and
derivative containing relatively little that reflects his own life experience. The past, ancient heroes, or mythical legends still seemed
infinitely more exciting and worthy of expression than his school
environment. Yet a deeply personal concern does at times creep into
several of his early stories and poems, especially those in which a
solitary figure heroically struggles against overwhelming odds. These
single-handed encounters no doubt suggest Reed's romantic inclinations as well as the direction that most of his reading had taken,
but they also hint at the sense of inadequacy he continued to feel
about meeting the expectations of his father. It is perhaps significant
that in "The Transformation" the ancient chief and father-figure
rewards the departing brave merely by saying: "Thou art a man,
my son" (6).

Harvard

Despite lingering concerns about parental acceptance that Reed
may have felt, he seems to have had no doubts whatsoever about
his writing abilities. He entered Harvard in the fall of 1906, eager
for literary acceptance. Such was the nature of his confidence that
after only a few days on campus he approached fellow classmate
Robert Hallowell with the proposal that they collaborate on a humorous book about Harvard. Hallowell, an artist, would provide
the sketches and Reed the text. When the astonished artist reminded
the aspiring writer that they had both just arrived and knew absolutely nothing about the university, Reed cavalierly dismissed
such concerns with a wave of the hand. "Hell," he replied, "we'll
find out doing the thing."[7] Despite such confidence, Reed quickly
discovered that eagerness did not always translate into success.

Although Reed knew his own literary skills, he wanted the campus to recognize them too. To his great pleasure, he found that the *Harvard Lampoon,* which appeared bimonthly and poked lighthearted fun at university institutions and campus life, accepted many of his contributions. Within a few months he was offering more than his share of jokes, satirical sketches, and doggerel. Typical of the kind of humor he submitted was the following verse aimed at a sister institution:

> When you see a Radcliffe maiden,
> With a pen and notebook laden
> Sneaking 'round the elm trees in the
>   yard some sunny April day.
> Don't demand an explanation
> For she's seeking information
> Which will soon be worked together in a
>   lifelike college play.
>
> (11)

Jack was somewhat less successful in achieving recognition for his other literary efforts, and it was not until the end of his freshman year that the more prestigious *Harvard Monthly,* a journal devoted to serious literature, accepted a poem and a short sketch. Although tied thematically to the kinds of poetry that he had written in Morristown, "Guinevere" is more mature in both concept and language, as its concluding stanza suggests:

> List to the awful kingly dirge; the sea
> Pours out his grieving heart with anguished wail
> Against the gray deserted cliffs, the while
> A dazzling presence shows its light to me;
> I, blinded whisper, "Art thou, the Grail?"
> And "Nay" it answers, "but the sad
>   queen's smile."
>
> (*Monthly,* June 1907, 11)

In "Bacchanal," which is more a tone poem than a story, the lost narrator encounters an ancient goddess of love after he has fallen asleep in a Greek ruin. The vision is as fleeting as is the story itself, and simply provided Reed an opportunity to display his descriptive talents. Later that summer while in Portland, Reed achieved further recognition when one of his poems was accepted by the *Pacific Monthly*.

Even though Jack's efforts at social acceptance during his second year at Harvard continued to flounder, he achieved considerably more success in his writing. Responsive to talent rather than social background or personal qualities, both the *Lampoon* and the *Monthly* elected him to their editorial boards; soon more of his work began to fill their pages. As his earliest biographer, Granville Hicks, remarked, during the remainder of his college career Reed was a prolific if not a terribly distinguished collegiate writer.[8] It must be remembered, however, that during this period a devotion to writing was not his only concern. Reed also filled his time with athletics, clubbing, and cheerleading. Busy as he was, Reed wrote quickly, revised little, and often used the first symbol or image that came to mind. Despite the pressures of campus life, he published over twenty poems, nine short stories, and wrote several plays or skits for various campus organizations.

Like many college writers, Reed experimented with different genres. His poetry was but one means by which he tested his literary skills. Although he liked to call himself a poet, Jack was never as fully commited to poetry as were others of his era. Reed was no Ezra Pound, who tried to write a sonnet a day while a student at the University of Pennsylvania, or an Alan Seeger who emotionally committed his life to poetry when he attended Harvard. He was caught up in too many activities to devote himself completely to any one of them. His poetic efforts at Harvard, which were but a part of his creative experimenting, might be separated into two broad categories: those poems that developed literary intentions and those that were essentially descriptive. The latter were often the most successful since they usually dealt with either familiar landscapes or phenomena from his western background. Perhaps recalling transcontinental trips across the country to and from college, he wrote "The Desert" during his sophomore year:

> Like ruins of some vast Titanic war
> The shattered desert lies, nor wakes the land
> Save in the storm, when at the god's command
> The mailed lightning shakes the rocky floor.
> All night the caravans of stars go by
> In silence. Still the sombre waste-land keeps

Its lonely watch while all the heaven sleeps,
And the lone moon is drowsy in the sky.
How delicate the trembling thrill that leaps
From heart to heart, as the pale star-
fires die!

(14)

If the mood and images in "The Desert" suggest the influence of Swinburne, Reed also shows here a greater confidence in his imagery. In fact, the longer he stayed in Cambridge, the more confident he became in describing his new surroundings. "A Winter Run," which he wrote during his junior year, is still traditional in versification, but Reed demonstrates an economy of language and a sharpening of his use of images in this set of quatrains:

Out of the warmth and the light
Into the frosty weather,
Into the teeth of a winter's night,
Running, we sprang together.

The icy, silent dark leapt up
And struck me in the face—
And the moon hung out her silver cup
As trophy for the race.

Our driving breath flung out behind
Like some dim, flying plume;
Our shadows, on the snow outlined,·
Ran with us in the gloom.

The long white road, the rhythmic beat
The wind-sword in our hair—
Oh, here's the spell of winged feet,
The charm of winter air!

(21)

Other poems like "Tschaikowsky," "The Tempest," and "The Traveler" were more formal and consciously literary as Reed tried to combine learning with creativity.

Reed was often willing to use a familiar setting for his poems, but not for his short stories. A sampling of these shows that they rarely deal with the present or familiar and often combine elements of the real with the surreal and supernatural. One exception is "The Red Hand" (*Monthly*, April 1908), written during his sophomore year. Set in Cambridge, this piece mirrors his frustrations with the social elitism that permeated campus life. The story hints of Poe in its mood and revenge motif. The narrator, who faces social exclusion and academic probation mandated by the college dean, is slowly drawn into a secret society made up of other collegiate outcasts. His roommate, Brodsky, a reminder of a Jewish roommate Reed shamefully abandoned his sophomore year, introduces him to the society, which consists of "a Chinaman, a negro, two or three men with Slavic features, and Merriman, whom I remembered as having been fired from college at the beginning of my Freshman year" (74). When the narrator drinks a glass of foul tasting substance, all inhibitions vanish and "in a moment I was talking, explaining my wrongs, and pleading eloquently with fiery denunciation of the Athletic Association, of the college, and of the Dean. I have never talked so brilliantly, and when I finished, my audience burst into a fierce cry of approbation" (74). Others too attacked the dean, a convenient symbol of all the university's inequities. They rolled a die and chose the narrator to destroy the common oppressor. The story's ending is left purposely vague. When the climactic event finally occurs, the narrator throws the bomb over the dean's shoulder towards Brodsky. In the explosion that follows it is not clear toward whom the bomb is thrown or how many imagined obstacles to success Reed had symbolically removed from the campus that he normally loved so well.

Much of the bitterness expressed in "The Red Hand" had subsided by Reed's junior year. By then his many activities and successes on the *Lampoon* and the *Monthly* had drawn him into campus life. His confidence in himself as a writer was also bolstered by his friendship with the professor of his English 12 class. Charles Townsend Copeland encouraged Reed's ambitions to write professionally and tried to sharpen his ability to observe. Bernard De Voto, also a Copeland student, recalled the professor's style: "Life was what he wanted— the things seen or heard, the thing felt, the experience of living men. He would rail at us from his desk in Emerson with the rhapsodic speech of Amos or Ezekiel. Look, the world was all around us and we ourselves were tumultuous with emotions begotten in it—why, then, did we persist in turning in to him pallid little violets from our reading?"[9] Much of Reed's work at this time hinted of the pallid little violet variety in setting and plot, but his descriptions sharpened and he developed more skillfully the mood and tone of each story. Description was his greatest strength. Reed's best writing was about a remembered landscape or familiar scene. Copeland had always encouraged this approach. But as happened with "From Clatsop to Nekarney" (*Monthly*, December 1908), Reed could lose control of his descriptive abilities. The story dealt with a camping trip that he and two friends had taken in Oregon. The scant narration is utterly overwhelmed by florid detail and dramatization of the ordinary. "The Pharaoh" (*Monthly*, January 1909), on the other hand, is set in Egypt during the time of the Second Dynasty. This story describes the Goddess Astarte's intervention in a revolution. She persuades the Pharaoh's high priest that fate has determined his master's overthrow. While the plot is scanty and melodramatic, Reed developed well a mood of foreboding doom.

One of Reed's more mature collegiate stories was written during the winter of his junior year. "The Singing Gates" (*Monthly*, February 1909) describes the growing madness of a lighthouse keeper who is driven to suicide by loneliness, an eerie environment, and the magical powers of a mysterious Indian god. As in most of Reed's early stories, there is virtually no character development, but the story has a convincing tone and the writing is among his best. "Dusk came, and as the sun let himself down into the sea, Jensen climbed the tower and lighted the lamp with nervous fingers. The fog had almost vanished and the birds with the singing voices had disappeared, but he could hear their cries high up, where they had lifted with the fog" (249).

During the rest of his college career, Reed found the time to write several more stories, including "The Winged Stone" (*Monthly*, April 1909), which contains the only autobiographical material that he ever published about his youth. Influenced as he was by the Arthurian legends, Reed has the hero in this story perform tasks that will give him special powers like Arthur. Once this is accomplished, the hero must choose between contentment or power and wealth. True to Reed's own ambitions, the hero selects the latter, although he is unable to keep what he has chosen. The other two stories Reed wrote during his frantically paced senior year are both ordinary and labored. "In England's Need" (*Monthly*, January and February 1910), about an English-French war and the return of Arthur, was the longest piece of fiction he attempted in college.

More plausible but no more successful is the weakly plotted and developed story, "East is East and West is West" (*Monthly*, October 1910), about warring factions of the Chinese Tong societies.

Somehow during his crowded senior year Reed also found time to write skits and short plays for campus organizations. His forays into drama are not particularly noteworthy, but represent yet another area in which he experimented with his writing. *Tit for Tat* was written for the Cosmopolitan Club and was based on the legend of the Tower of Babel.[10] In the play, male bosses are confronted by outraged female workers who demand the right to vote. All ends well when both men and women form a union against the tower's contractors. Also during his senior year the elitist Hasty Pudding Club pleased Jack greatly by asking him to write the lyrics for their annual musical comedy. Reed collaborated with two other students to write and produce *Diana's Debut*.[11] The play is a musical farce describing the debut of the Turkish sultan's daughter. It demonstrates little more than Reed's eagerness to be a part of the campus elite even if it were only his writing skills that were in demand. His final contribution to the dramatic arts was a thirteen-page skit, *The Last of the Pirates*.[12] This work, even more banal than what he had previously written, was performed at one of the traditional evenings before graduation ceremonies.

After four years at Harvard, Reed had written a great deal, but little of genuine quality. Nevertheless, his college years gave him the chance to hone his skills by experimenting widely in different genres. Besides what he wrote for campus consumption, Reed worked on many other projects. Among his unpublished manuscripts is an outline for a novel, parts of several plays, unfinished poems, and various other fragments.[13] This work suggests that Reed was serious about his writing, that he enjoyed it, and did it regularly. It also suggests that he wrote rapidly and engaged in little revision, for writing was but a part of his activity-filled collegiate career. As he made ready to leave Cambridge, he wrote two last poems, which reflected his view of the future. "Willamette" is a nostalgic work in which Reed combines childhood memories and uncertainties about what lies ahead:

> Long, long ago
> Still did the eerie morn
> Pale the dark stream and edge the pines with fire

Ere yet was born
The star-white city of my birth
And my desire,
The garden-spot of earth.
And through the night
Still came the sound of singing, as you passed
Proudly and strong, to join yourself at last
To the Columbia, against the sea,
Great leader of a hopeless cause eternally.

(30)

"Wanderlust," which he wrote shortly before graduation, suggests the lure of new horizons:

For the sea calls to go forth to the sea and
world's far ending,
And the gull's cry carries the sound of gongs from
the temples of Ind,
And the phantoms of wanderers suffer from lust and
desire unending,
Luring with scent of strange flowers caught in the
hair of the wind.

(29–30)

The new horizons that beckoned John Reed were but a short train ride from the streets of Cambridge to New York.

A Poet in New York

With graduation and five months of European travel behind him, Reed came to New York in the spring of 1911, determined to make his way as a writer. The job provided by Steffens on the *American* paid his living expenses while he learned the realities of the New York literary world. During the next two years, as Reed continued to experiment widely with a variety of literary forms, he also continued to view himself primarily as a poet. From the spring of 1911 through 1913, he wrote more poetry than during any other period of his life. Reed quickly learned that poets did not earn much money. He also discovered that commercial magazines had little interest in poetry of any kind and paid little for the few poems they published. The problem as he saw it was the commercialization of the arts and the deadening middle-class ethos that permeated the country. After six months of Village life, he sent a letter to Harriet Monroe, the editor of *Poetry*, a new magazine of verse in Chicago, in which he explained the real reason for poetry's fall from popularity: "I am myself on the staff of a magazine, and have often heard the editors say that poetry was a declining art. The reasons they gave might interest you as they did me: 'That the public had lost the appreciation of rhythm, because verse was no longer spoken or sung; and that the printed poem conveyed no sense of melody to those who read only with the eye.' " This explanation distorted the issue and prematurely banished poetry to the fringes of literary expression. Reed argued that the true poet was still very much in demand. "And I have found that among men of whatever class, if they are deeply stirred by emotion, poetry appeals; as indeed all the arts appeal. The apathetic, mawkishly-religious middle class are our enemies."[14]

If Reed attacked the poet's enemy, his literary animosity did not usually influence his work. Much of his verse during this period reflected a sense of discovery rather than revolt. His New York poetry abandoned the myths and legends of his college years and focused instead on his own impressions. New York City enthralled him and the present now seemed as worthy of acknowledgment as the past. Reed's early efforts showed more thematic than structural changes. Although traditional in form, "The Foundations of a Skyscraper," published by the *American* in October 1911, demonstrates a new urban orientation in imagery and firmness in the use of language:

> Clamor of unknown tongues, and hiss or arc,
> Clashing and blending; screech of wheel on wheel,—
> Naked, a giant's back, tight-muscled, stark,
> Glimpse of mighty shoulder, etched in steel.
> And over all, above the highest high,
> A phantom of fair towers in the sky.
>
> (33)

Reed also replaced another of his early themes, the emptiness of the West, with a focus on the fullness of the city. "A Hymn to Manhattan," for example, compares in heroic couplets New York to other great cities that symbolized the dominance of an entire civilization:

> Here's all of Europe in one place;
> Beauty unconscious, yes, and even grace.
> Rome? Here all that Rome was, and is not;
> Here Babylon—and Babylon's forgot.
> Golden Byzantium, drunk with pride and sin,
> Carthage, that flickered out where we begin. . . .
> London? A swill of mud in Shakespear's time;
> Ten Troys lie tombed in centuries of grime!
>
> (45)

Yet this hymn of praise ends on an equivocal note. Suggesting his own ambiguous feelings about urban values, Reed was unsure whether as a symbol of America New York's great physical growth was attended by a sense of grandeur:[15]

> Ah, that is how she sings!
> Wake to the visions shining in the sun;
> Earth's ancient, conquering races rolled into one,
> A world beginning—*and yet nothing done!*
>
> (45)

Although the city continued to influence Reed's poetic consciousness, he did not completely lose his romantic fascination with the heroic glories of the past. He creatively merged past and present when he completed "Sangar" in 1911, the longest poem he had yet attempted. Written in traditional ballad form, the poem was inspired by Lincoln Steffens's failed efforts to reconcile labor and management in Los Angeles. When Reed could find no commercial outlet for the poem, he sent it to Harriet Monroe in Chicago. She helped place the piece in the December 1912 issue of *Poetry.* "Sangar" was chosen as one of the ten best poems accepted by the magazine that year. Monroe called the poem "an old-form ballad with a modern meaning."[16]

Reed drew his inspiration for "Sangar" from Steffens's coverage of the Los Angeles trial of the McNamara brothers of the Ironworkers Union. They were charged with a bombing of the antilabor *Los Angeles Times,* in which twenty-one people had been killed. The trial had polarized the city, pitting one class against another. Hoping to defuse an explosive situation and save the McNamaras' lives, Steffens tried to arrange a plea bargain for the defendants. But when the well-intentioned plan went awry, labor leaders damned him for interfering.

Reed wrote "Sangar" as a tribute to his friends' noble failure. A romantic allegory, the poem describes a medieval battle in which the mighty warrior Sangar and his son are called upon to fight once again against invading barbarians. With the enemy defeated and surrounded, Sangar tried to stop the fighting in the interest of Christian brotherhood. But the slaughter continues when Sangar's hot-tempered son denounces his father as a traitor and kills him. Like Steffens, Sangar had failed to transcend the fury of human passions. His reward would be found elsewhere:

> Oh, there was joy in Heaven when Sangar came.
> Sweet Mary wept, and bathed and bound his wounds,
> And God the Father healed him of despair,
> And Jesus gripped his hand, and laughed and
> laughed. . . .
>
> (43)

Reed probably did not intend it, but Steffens ultimately viewed the poem as a form of rebuke.[17]

Shortly before "Sangar" appeared in print, Reed suffered a deeply felt personal loss. His father died in the summer of 1912, and he had to return to Portland to settle family matters. What he planned as a temporary visit home turned into a three-month stay as Jack dealt with a perplexing number of family financial problems. He finally returned to New York in October, carrying with him the best and most sustained piece of work that he had yet done. The stay in Portland had caused him to miss Village life. In *The Day in Bohemia, or Life among the Artists* he tried to recapture the atmosphere of the Village literary world. The poem is a long, witty, satirically loving *tranche de vie* of all the foibles, pretensions, and general good times of this American bohemia. Unlike a later generation of self-proclaimed nonconformists, *The Day in Bohemia* lacks the bitterness of Alen Ginsberg's *Howl,* or the ultimate seriousness of many of Jack Kerouac's novels. Instead it is a playful ode to joy in which the poet shows his abilities at satire, parody, and rollicking characterization. Something like the skits he produced at Harvard, *The Day in Bohemia* was far better and more mature in both design and workmanship.

The poem describes a typical day in the lives of Reed and his roommates at 42 Washington Square South, whose creative abilities are still unsung:

> I would embalm in deathless rhyme
> The great souls of our little time:
> Inglorious Miltons by the score,—
> Mute Wagners—Rembrandts, ten or more,—
> And Rodins, one to every floor.
> In short, those unknown men of genius
> Who dwell in third-floor-rears gangreneous,
> Reft of their rightful heritage
> By a commercial, soulless age.
>
> (11)

Reed catalogues the inconveniences of a New York walk-up, which the would-be artists cheerfully endure, then parodies how other poets (Shelley, Maeterlinck, Keats, Whitman), might have described the neighbor's wash that he sees from his bedroom window.

With that heroic atmosphere established, the day itself begins with customary bantering and horseplay. As a result, everyone is late for work. When Reed arrives at the office of the *American* in mid-morning, future literary ambitions and analytical discussion take the place of editorial work. At lunch the poet-narrator gathers with other writers and editors for the weekly meeting of the literary Dutch Treat Club. More discussions and literary arguments fill the early afternoon until they all reluctantly return to their jobs. As the workday ends, the poet hurries off to an "aesthetic tea" hosted by the painter, UMBILLICUS who has affected all of the artistic trappings except that of actually painting. Throughout the early evening, an unceasing flow of "neo-Bohemian dubs," whom the poet detests, continue to eddy in the sullied atmosphere of this pretentious gathering:

> A clack of squabbling voices smites the ear.
> Dim in the murk the other cranks appear;
> BUFO, who one short verse per year produces,
> Explaining by the following excuses:
> "I Youth's sweet-scented manuscript unroll,
> "But when the heart's systole and diastole
> "O'erflows the well of poetry in my soul."

(BUFO's an Art-for-Art's-sake out-and-outer,—
We're fortunate his well is not a spouter)
TRIMALCHIO, long-haired, who thinks it nice is
That artists should be steeped in all the vices;
And measures such a man, not by his wits,
But by th' atrocities that he commits
Hates decency as Ghibelline a Guelph,—
Not brave enough to either be, himself;
STREPHON, who sings of Youth, and Wind, and Flowers,
And open Roads, and Vagabonds, for hours;
Cries "Back to Nature," goes without a hat,
And—never stirs from his steam-heated flat!
Anear him CHLOE, in a pastoral dress,—
Which cost at least three hundred flat, I guess,—
Revolves her onyx eyes with some success;
She wields no brush, manipulates no lyre,
Her job in life is simply to Inspire.

(30–31)

The poet finally escapes from the tea and the Village types to race
back into the city where life and beauty are real, where true art is
found. He spends the rest of the night with friends engaged in
honest discussions about life, art, the world.

By the time Reed wrote *The Day in Bohemia,* the Village had
replaced Harvard as the center of his world, but his race for glory
continued. Reed still took poetry and the arts most seriously and
he diligently pursued the real work of writing. Yet he continued
to live his life as fully and joyfully as possible. If the city was
beginning to touch Reed's social conscience, he was still the carefree
poet who desperately wanted to make a name for himself. Thus,
The Day in Bohemia not only captures his own moods and ambitions,
it also suggests the joyful season of revolt that characterized Village
life during the prewar period.

The Day in Bohemia did not appear in print until February 1913,
when a small press in Connecticut privately published five hundred
copies. The Village provided his most appreciative audience, and
Jack enjoyed the recognition the poem brought him. Immodest as
ever, he distributed it himself, often selling copies for a dollar.
Although he never stopped writing poems, his next book of verse
did not appear until 1917. All but three of the twenty-five poems
in *Tamburlaine* (1917) had been written either during or before the

period 1911–14. Reed stated in a foreword that he hoped the volume would be considered "a combination of a First Book of Verse, and a collection of Juvenilia." While he expected other books of verse to follow, except for a handful of poems, the verse in *Tamburlaine* marked the conclusion rather than the beginning of a poetic career. In later years, Jack regretted that his political activities took him away from his poetry. In the summer of 1919, when he had to leave a lovely Cape Cod setting to keep political promises, he lamented to his friends, "Maybe it will surprise you, but what I really want is to write poetry."[18] Reed seemed to want to get back to writing poetry, but after his early New York period, he was always more of a poet in mind than in fact. He certainly had the sensitivity of a poet, and his descriptive abilities were those of a poet, but even when he was producing most of his poetry he continued to write more prose than verse. In comparison with other American poets of the period—T.S. Eliot, Ezra Pound, or William Carlos Williams—Reed seemed only to dabble in poetry. As one critic suggests, the Village community of writers was divided between those who experimented with modern forms of writing and those who did not.[19] Reed the poet was never particularly interested in new techniques. He began his poetic career using conventional forms like the sonnet and ballad. Once in New York he moved toward a kind of verse that was more closely tied to prose. Yet the modern turn of his poetic diction probably did not result from any conscious decision on his part. Reed was more likely influenced by his work on the *American* and by his writing of more and more prose. As a poet, Reed never truly found a voice of his own. His poetry remained largely derivative as he tried one style after another. He was most often at his best when he cared less about writing messages and more about being a singer and image-maker. Not surprisingly, when he tried the hardest his poetry was the most contrived. Ultimately, his poetic skills served him best when he used them as a journalist to produce brilliantly descriptive prose.

Essays, Stories, and Sketches

When Reed first arrived in New York, Lincoln Steffens advised him to experiment with his life and career before settling into any permanent mold. Fully aware of Jack's preference for poetry, Steffens also did not want him to channel his talents in one direction.

Writing to Reed in the spring of 1911, Steffens defended his own
writing style by arguing that "poetry is not more romantic than
prose can be. Indeed, I've known them to become not only engaged,
but married, happily."[20] Eventually the two merged in much of
Reed's writing, but in the spring of 1911, prose was still his work,
poetry his passion. Over the next year and a half, as Reed came to
know New York, he tried to interpret his experiences through both
mediums. Reed's life in New York was no calmer than in his Harvard
days, a fact that was sometimes reflected in his work. Indeed,
Steffens warned him that he wrote too fast.[21] Yet Reed's ideas for
poems, plays, stories, and novels always seemed more numerous
than the hours in a day. So confident of his abilities, he was rarely
bashful about trying to get his work accepted. When he first arrived
in New York he tried without success to capitalize on his European
trip by selling an article entitled "A Dash into Spain" and a short
story describing the Reed-Peirce misadventures aboard the cattle
boat. The mounting stacks of rejection slips failed to daunt his
enthusiasm. Reed continued to write and send his work out. His
early publishing successes, modest as they were, still came after
only a relatively short period of failure. By the end of 1911, he had
published four articles and two stories. These articles were techni-
cally proficient but offered no hint of Reed's future accomplishments
or interests. "The Immigrants," for example, published in the May
issue of *Collier's* (20 May 1911) was a brief, naive, and ornate prose
poem proclaiming the golden opportunities that awaited new arrivals
to American shores. A month later, an allegory, "The Involuntary
Ethics of Big Business," appeared in *Trend* (June 1911), and although longer it was as stilted in concept and argumentation. In
this piece Reed contended that American businessmen, despite their
profit motives, still contributed through their activities to the public
good. Here Reed continued to defend the status quo as he had done
so often at Harvard. Two articles appearing later that fall in the
American were considerably better, for both dealt with subjects familiar to Reed. "A Reminiscence" (November 1911) briefly describes a chance encounter he had had with William James in
Cambridge. His sketch of Charles Townsend Copeland (November
1911)—a labor of love—captured the uniqueness of his old Harvard
professor.

Harvard was still very much on Jack's mind in 1912. With the
approval of the editors of the *American,* he undertook an ambitious

research project to analyze how Harvard "connected up with the world once more."[22] Reed produced a long article that was much more radical than any of his college work. He praised the growing awareness of faculty and students of the political and social issues outside campus life and defended the students' demand for an open speakers policy against administrative opposition. While the article exaggerated the importance of this "Harvard Renaissance," it was well researched and written. Unfortunately, it was also too long and radical for the editors at the *American*. Supporting the student viewpoint was one thing, but calling attention to the conservative perspective of the university's governing board was too controversial, and the article was never published. Angered by what he saw as commercial restraints on publishers, Reed poured his frustrations into a three-page manifesto, "Art for Art's Sake." Here he argued fervently that a "real artist goes on creating for art's sake whether he achieves publication or not."[23]

The *American* published three other noncontroversial articles by Reed. Two rather perfunctory biographies appeared in the "Interesting People" section (April, October 1912). The third piece, entitled "The Dinner Guests of Big Tim" (December 1912), described the Christmas Day dinner that Tammany boss Big Tim Sullivan gave for the Bowery bums in 1911. This was Reed's longest piece of reporting to date. No routine work of journalism, the article reflects a poet's eye as Reed describes the nuances of the holiday affair in which the city's forgotten and defeated found temporary relief. He contrasts the derelicts stumbling up the dingy stairway into the banquet hall where tables were heaped with food, with Big Tim's helpers who bullied them along: "Slide up, grandpa! What the hell are you standing there for? Keep your hats on! This ain't anybody's parlor" (103). Yet Reed's romantic nature led him to focus on the human warmth that flowed beneath the surface of this sad setting. "As I passed down the dark stairs," he wrote, "I met a shadowy, blotched line moving wearily up. It had waited long, this line. It was dreary, and dull, and silent; but it had life: it moved—up" (104).

If the Big Tim article and other Reed short stories were sentimental, they could also be full of life. Indeed, it was the honestly detailed way Reed described New Yorkers who lived on the edge of social respectability that first caught the attention of Max Eastman. But Jack had only gradually come to know this side of city life, and he drew upon other subjects for his early stories. His account of his shipboard adventures, for example, eventually appeared in print after he sold the rights to the established writer Julian Street. The *Saturday Evening Post* published the tale under both their names (28 October 1911). Several months earlier the *Forum* had accepted another story, "The Swimmers" (August 1911). This was the kind of eerie tale reminiscent of Reed's writing at Harvard. A shipwrecked swimmer in the middle of the Pacific encounters another, much older swimmer of Oriental origin who warns the young American that life in the East is different. Paying no attention to this admonition, the young swimmer expends all his energy pursuing a mirage, and thus hastening his own doom. Although the plot flows smoothly, Reed does not fully analyze the differences between East and West nor does he develop the story well. The next year (June, September 1912) *Century* magazine published two of his stories, each more lighthearted, longer, and polished than earlier efforts. Set in Paris, these stories describe the activities of a baker turned detective, Monsieur Vidoq. Lacking ability or common sense, he blunders into solving crimes. Although several notches above his college writing, neither tale is particularly absorbing or subtle in plot or character development.

"Where the Heart Is," which he wrote towards the middle of 1912, was far superior to anything Reed had yet done and demonstrated his developing sensitivity as a writer.[24] This story also shows the growing influence of the city on his fiction, poetry, and journalism. It is a simple yet intriguing tale about a New York dance hall girl who saves her money to broaden her horizons by traveling to Europe. When her funds run out after only a week abroad, she is forced to live by her wits. She takes up with a variety of male companions who pay her way while she continues to enjoy the sights. Eventually, she follows a lover to Rio and lives there in luxury until she becomes homesick for the sounds and smells of "old honest, low brow New York" (*Masses,* January 1913, 9). In a reversal of the Jamesian theme, she rejects the culture of the Old World for the sordid but familiar surroundings of the dance hall— the only place she truly feels at home. Unlike the sentimental Big Tim article, "Where the Heart Is" is narrated in a straightforward manner without patronizing the characters or moralizing the situation. No doubt influenced by O. Henry, whom he admired, Reed still refused to end the story on a moralistic note.[25] For this reason none of the commercial magazines would accept it, putting him once again in the position of writing for art's sake. "Where the Heart Is" eventually appeared in the *Masses*, a magazine always willing to experiment, to invite rather than to avoid controversy.

By the end of 1912, when Reed first discovered the *Masses*, he was nearing the end of his apprenticeship as a writer. He still had much to learn and much of the skill apparent in his later works was not yet evident. Yet, by the end of 1912, Reed as a writer had advanced far beyond his prep school and college days. Turning away from the mythical past for subject matter, he began to study his own environment. His love of adventure and his impetuousness aided him in this respect, for he was never content to live the experiences of others. Reed's life in New York helped to transform his creative vision as he began observing, and then describing the city of which he had become so much a part. At the same time Reed's enormous ego led him to write his thoughts hurriedly and then to pursue publishers aggressively. Much of his work at this time he did quickly without discipline. Noting this, his friend Lincoln Steffens advised him to slow down and pay more attention to perfecting his writing. But Jack was always too busy, too involved in sampling new experiences, too caught up in the process of living to be a careful craftsman. It was fortunate for him that writing usually came easily. By 1912, he had shown his ability to write, but he had yet to produce a great work. Indeed, there was little in his writing that suggested the direction his career would take. His Big Tim article, for example, may have been an excellent piece of reportage, but it still lacked the excitement, the descriptive brilliance, and the sense of personal commitment that so marks his later writing. To this point in his life, Jack had focused on developing his own career. But now, while his personal needs remained important, his social conscience—awakened by his New York experiences—began to develop. "Where the Heart Is," for example, not only reflected a more controlled prose and a more highly developed narrative technique, but also suggested a growing social awareness relatively free of sentimentalism or paternalistic compassion. By the end of 1912 most of his writer's technical skills were in place. What Reed needed now was an event that would join together observation, participation, and a personal sense of commitment. Such an event occurred in Paterson, New Jersey.

Chapter Four
The Writer as Observer

From January 1913 when his work first began appearing in the *Masses,* until he left for the Russian Revolution in September 1917, John Reed enjoyed one of the most productive periods of his life. During this time he published *Insurgent Mexico, The War in Eastern Europe,* a book of verse, four plays, over twenty short stories and sketches, three dozen articles in addition to those collected in his books, and close to sixty signed newspaper reports. He also wrote his unpublished autobiographical essay "Almost Thirty." Yet there were periods during these years when Reed lapsed into a despondent lethargy, worrying about the future and writing little. One such period came in the wake of the Paterson Pageant. Reed tried to forget the money that was lost by rushing off to Italy with Mabel Dodge. For the next six months, which he spent in the Villa Curonia or in Dodge's Fifth Avenue apartment, Reed enjoyed himself but continued to feel guilty about failing the workers. During this period he felt little commitment to anything and he found little he thought was worth writing about. As depressing as this creative dry spell was for Reed, it was brief. A chance to go to Mexico set his pen once again to work. There a sense of adventure, a shared commitment, and a desire to describe what he was seeing renewed his creative energy.

Another even bleaker period in Reed's life occurred just before he left for Russia in 1917. Illness, marital problems, disgust with the war, and difficulty in writing all dragged him down. Just as the Mexican venture had, his Russian trip gave new life to his creative energies. But Reed never again became the popular journalist of earlier years. His antiwar views closed off commercial outlets for publication. His enthusiasm for the Bolshevik cause ensured that these outlets would never be open to him again. Yet Reed had often found commercial publishers resistant to his work. Granville Hicks suggests that he did two kinds of writing: the kind that editors liked and the kind that he liked.[1] This was certainly true of the short stories he produced during these years, for many of those he liked best appeared in the *Masses* rather than in the better-known commercial magazines for which they were unsuited.

Short Stories and Sketches

Of the twenty-one stories and sketches Reed published during this period, half were in the *Masses*. The rest appeared in such periodicals as *Smart Set, Collier's, Metropolitan,* and *Century.* No collection of his stories was published until after his death.[2] Nearly all of the stories and sketches that Reed wrote from 1913 to 1917 can be divided into four thematic categories: sketches with New York as setting, humorous tales based on improbable or exaggerated situations, stories influenced by his Mexican adventures, or stories relating to World War I.

Most of Reed's New York sketches are relatively brief slices of life, examining the world of bums, prostitutes, and others adrift in the city. In his best fiction of this time, the present largely eclipses the past. Reed's own experiences now seem worthy of literary expression. Consequently, in many of these sketches and stories he is both observer and participant. Life in New York taught him to listen. In the best of these stories, Reed captures the idiomatic hopes and fears of shop girls, panhandlers, and various other city dwellers struggling to keep their dignity in a cruel world. The city is a protean blend of good and evil, pleasure and tragedy. Missing from these stories is the heavy sentimentalism of his earlier efforts. Now Reed is more sophisticated and ironic in handling human tragedy.

"A Taste of Justice" (*Masses*, April 1913) is typical of Reed's New York sketches. In this autobiographical piece, he demonstrates the ironic two-sided nature of the law. As Reed watches a group of prostitutes on their nightly patrol, he notices that as long as they keep moving the cop on the beat leaves them alone. This charade continues until Reed the observer is discovered and warned to stop loitering. When he refuses to move, he is hauled off to night court where he finds several of the prostitutes awaiting a hearing. A young woman who precedes him is automatically sentenced to ten days for soliciting. But when the judge recognizes Jack Reed, he chastises the sullen cop for arresting him and invites Reed to join him on the bench. Having nothing but contempt for such hypocrisy, Reed still lacked an ideology that could explain or rectify what he had observed. What he could do, however, was write about it.

The more Reed wandered about the city, the more conscious he became of his own privileged position. In "Another Case of Ingratitude" (*Masses*, July 1913), he satirized the self-serving motivations behind middle-class humanitarian concerns. The story describes Reed's encounter with a bum leaning against a building asleep on his feet. Reed took him to a restaurant, gave him money for a room, and then plied him with questions about his past. In no mood to discuss his personal life, the bum ridiculed Reed's impulse for helping him: " 'But if you hadn't struck me, you'd 'a' hunted up another down-and-outer. You see,' he leaned across the table, explaining. 'You just had to save somebody tonight. I understand. I got a appetite like that, too. Only mine's women' " (17). Here Reed expresses a theme that appears time and again in later works—the poor do not exist for the convenience of writers who may, in fact, be less aware of human foibles than their oppressed subjects.

Reed's growing awareness of the mutable nature of city life is best exemplified in a story entitled "Seeing is Believing" (*Masses*, December 1913). The story revolves around a series of encounters between a well-to-do, cynical, New Yorker named George and a seventeen-year-old girl from Chillicothe, Ohio, who has saved her money for six years in order to see the city. By the time they meet she is adrift without any means of support but confident that she will find someone to help her. George is convinced that she is a prostitute until her innocence persuades him that her story is true. He gives her money when she promises to go home. Three weeks later they meet again and his sardonic accusations are again parried by her implausible yet childlike explanations. George gives her money a second time. At the story's end, he is unable to figure her out. Like Robin in "My Kinsman, Major Molineux," Reed too is learning that in the city nothing is as it seems. Seeing is not always believing, or is it? "Broadway Night" (*Masses*, May 1916) is a more complex sketch in which Reed toys with the counterpointal impact of the city on the lives of its citizens. The story begins as Reed chats with an elderly man reduced to selling the *Matrimonial News* among the swarms of pleasure seekers and providers on Broadway. He hears a story of profound tragedy—the death of a wife and two children and the loss of a job to the efficiency craze. As the two men talk, an overweight, aging prostitute buys a paper for the hope it offers and the entertainment it provides on Sunday, her only day off. The story ends with Reed and a young streetwalker "kissing hotly" and dancing to the wild syncopation of two orchestras in a local supper club. Reed adroitly portrays the city as an indifferent blend of cruelty and excitement. He is as nonjudgmental about the lives he observes as the down-and-out hawker of the *Matrimonial News* who declares: "As for you, I suppose you'll go helling about with drink and women. . . . Well, go your ways. I'm past blaming anyone for anything!" (20). New York could be fun to some and brutal to others. Reed's supper club companion, who had never read a newspaper or known much about the outside world, seemed to feel at home in her part of the city. "How perfectly she was mistress of her world!" (20). Reed had mastered his world as well. Yet life in New York remained a jungle of uncertainty, as he suggests to another prostitute earlier in the story: "This . . . is what they call Natural Selection!" (20).

Unlike the stories published in the *Masses,* most of the fiction Reed wrote for commercial outlets avoided controversial subjects. Consequently, the exaggerated humor that pervaded his prep school and college work often resurfaced in his commercial pieces. In his two Grampus Bill stories, "The Cook and the Captain Bold" (*Metropolitan,* November 1914) and "The Buccaneer's Grandson" (*Metropolitan,* January 1917), and in "The Peripatetic Prince" (*Smart Set,* June 1913), the formula is essentially the same. In each story, larger-than-life characters engaged in improbable escapades that never turn out as expected. For the most part, these are unexceptional pieces that show nothing more than Reed's ability to write for money.

Conversely, the two stories Reed wrote at this time about his Mexican experiences merit closer examination. "Mac-American" (*Masses,* April 1914) and "Endymion: or On the Border" (*Masses,* December 1916), like most of the city sketches, are based on his own observations. "Mac-American"—more a character sketch than a story—is about a drifter and brawler Reed met in Chihuahua City who symbolized American contempt for Mexicans and their revolution. Rebuking the Mexicans for their filth and immorality, Mac relates his own life story of deceit, bigotry, and violence. Blind to such hypocrisy, he declares, "I wouldn't like to live down here in Mexico. . . . The people haven't got any Heart. I like people to be friendly, like Americans" (9). Reed makes it clear that Mac is no different from the many other Americans he had met in Mexico.

With their ugly nationalism and predatory instincts, their only goal was the pursuit of the dollar. For these "friendly Americans," Mexico was a country to be exploited.

Reed's other Mexican sketch, "Endymion," describes a different kind of drifter whose self-destructive temperament does not extend to those around him. The central character is Doc, a London-trained surgeon, now a tramp and hopeless alcoholic. Doc's decline followed the tragic death of his wife who once inscribed a book of poetry to him as her Endymion. Old and battered by life, Doc has developed, through his own suffering, a kindred bond with others whose lives are no better than his own—poor Mexicans, saddle-tramps, and derelicts. Like Raskolnikov's, Doc's personal shame leads him to empathize with others. While he fails to earn the love of a goddess as Endymion does, through his humanitarianism he earns the admiration of those around him.

Besides his Mexican stories, Reed also produced six stories with World War I as a setting. Two of these appeared almost a year apart in the *Metropolitan*. "The Englishman: A War Correspondent's Wondering Observation" (*Metropolitan*, October 1914) was based on a rail trip across the United States that Reed made during the early months of the war. He shared a coach with a polite, but aloof young Englishman hurrying back home to enlist. Reed describes his companion's indifference to the causes of the war and his neutral feelings about Germany. The young man was going home because of his family's military involvement and because, to put it simply, it was the thing to do. To Reed, such shallow reasoning was little different than the absurd arguments the belligerents used to vindicate their stance.

"The Barber of Lille" (*Metropolitan*, July 1915), another World War I piece, differs from many Reed stories of this period in that it was purely imaginative. Thematically similar to William Dean Howells's "Editha," Reed's tale also concerns a woman who goads a man into taking a stand for his country. Set in German-occupied France, the tale is about Madeleine Pouvier, who is married to a barber, Ferdinand. Enraged by the failure of her town to expel the Germans, she is convinced that a symbolic gesture will spark the needed action. Pouvier urges her husband to kill the next German who sits in his barber chair. Faced with his wife's contempt and thoughts of his own cowardice, Ferdinand cuts the throat of a dashing young German who happens to be his wife's lover. Only the story's ending saves it from pure melodrama. The townspeople do nothing because German money has made their lives too comfortable. Here Reed shows the insanity and corruption of both sides as they do damage to each other.

"Daughter of the Revolution" (*Masses,* February 1915), also set in wartime France, is one of Reed's best stories. Longer and more complex than most of his other fiction in the *Masses,* it focuses on a Parisian prostitute, Marcelle, who relates her life's story to a group of American soldiers. Beginning with her grandfather, who was shot as a Communard, three generations of her family were revolutionaries. At once proud and ashamed of her heritage, she too has fought for her freedom, but in a different way. The family poverty caused by her father's radicalism affects her deeply. Her great desire is to be free from this misery to enjoy life's luxuries. But she cannot escape her heritage. Like the rest of her family, she will not take orders from bosses or supervisors nor will she work as a wage slave in a factory. Marcelle turns to prostitution as the best way of realizing her dream of freedom. While her father rejects her, Marcelle's brother understands her radicalism and realizes that they are both seeking a different kind of freedom. Her rebellion was personal, the kind with which Reed was most comfortable. Like Marcelle, he too was a radical but one still closely tied to the Village ethos of freeing the individual from smothering middle-class constraints.

Nearly all Reed's best stories of these years appeared in the *Masses.* They represent the kind of writing that he liked to do rather than the kind that the commercial press liked to print. Cast as fiction, these sketches and stories are the vignettes of a journalist who embellishes his observations and personal encounters. Character development is missing from even the best of them. The plots are simple or nonexistent. Yet beneath the surface realities are complex human predicaments. Time and again the narrator, often Reed himself, discovers subtleties about the lives of his characters that give added twists to unresolved conclusions. The tone and subject matter of many of the *Masses* stories and their often unexpected endings suggest the influence of O. Henry. In addition, a familiarity with Stephen Crane can be noted in Reed's sparse style, in the nature of his urban imagery, his frequent contrasts between high and low characters, and in the subjectivity of the viewer/narrator.[3] While Reed is less detached than Crane from his subject matter, he also has learned to clothe his anger in irony. And while he portrays the dregs of society as humorously and humanely as O. Henry, and the realities of urban existence as unflinchingly as Crane, Reed tends to focus his ridicule more on the nature of the system than on the naiveté or flaws of his characters. Even when he wrote fiction, Reed's best work was linked to reality. Fiction generated by his own sensitive observations could be quite good. Stories that relied solely on his imagination could be wooden and contrived. His subject matter came to life in proportion to his closeness to it. In everything that Reed produced—poetry, articles, fiction, and plays—this was always true.

Launching a Career in Paterson

Reed's description of the Paterson Strike ("War in Paterson," *Masses,* June 1913) dramatically displayed his literary skills. In Paterson he found the perfect subject for his pen—a collective struggle against injustice. Reed showed in his opening sentence that no ordinary labor-management dispute was taking place: "There's a war in Paterson. But it's a curious kind of war. All the violence is the work of one side—the Mill Owners" (14). "War in Paterson" is more than the story of a strike. Modern industrial warfare is the central theme described sharply and subjectively. Reed the author is a participant in the battle who shares the strikers' goals as he is initiated into the realities of class conflict.

In the first half of the article, Reed establishes the setting for the strike. The police bully the workers, Reed is arrested for refusing to move from a striker's porch, and he is sentenced, through a jaded legal process, to twenty days in jail. Here the reader learns as much about Reed's activities in Paterson as about the strike itself. Only when Reed describes his jail experiences do the real participants in the strike emerge. There he meets many workers, most of them immigrants, who share with him their hardships and commitments. Reed had earlier outlined how local government officials, the police, and the press had united against the strikers. In his jail cell he learned that the strikers expected such opposition. Indeed, they saved their most bitter denunciation for less obvious class enemies such as the English-speaking workers who had shunned the strike, the local clergy, the leadership of the AF of L, and even the Socialist party, which had found them too radical. Yet it was precisely the strikers' radicalism that Reed found so attractive. The courage and dedication of this strange mixture of immigrant workers and Wobbly leaders left him enthralled: "Think of it! Twelve years they have been losing strikes—twelve solid years of disappointments and incalculable suffering. They must not lose again! They cannot lose!" (17). Committed as he was to the success of the strike, Reed was not content to end the article with a stirring editorial comment. Instead he placed the workers once again at the center stage. Unlike most of them, he was released from jail just four days after his arrest. Imprisoned strike leaders like Bill Haywood were helped by union lawyers to obtain quick release and continue their work. Only the strikers themselves remained in jail. Yet they felt no bitterness or frustration. " 'You go out,' they said softly. 'Thass nice. Glad you go out. Pretty soon we go out. Then we go back on picket-line' " (17). This kind of courage and determination thrilled Reed. When he left the Paterson jail he planned to carry the spirit of the strikers to those who had not been fortunate enough to be in Paterson to observe it for themselves.

Reed closed "War in Paterson" with the same kind of dramatic flair that marked its opening sentence. While learning the realities of this industrial struggle he had been converted. His article transformed the Paterson strike into a morality play. The forces of good and evil were clear. Reed enhanced the dramatic effect by saying little about the cause of the strike or the setting, by including only material that added to the dramatic mood. Nowhere does he write, for example, that his cell-mates mistook him for a police spy until Bill Haywood recognized him. Nor does Reed discuss the prisoners he met who had nothing to do with the strike. Rather, "War in Paterson" is the story of imprisoned strikers and their remarkable solidarity.

A fuller description of Reed's experience in the Paterson jail can be found in "Sheriff Radcliff's Hotel," an article published in the *Metropolitan,* September 1913. Here Reed is writing for public consumption, for those more interested in muckraking than in radicalism. While scarcely mentioning the strike, he condemns conditions in the jail. He also describes the emotionally disturbed, the petty criminals, and the bums who are all locked up together because no one knows what else to do with them. In this article Reed is more an observer than a participant. He describes rather than identifies with his fellow prisoners. Pity rather than solidarity is the controlling motif. The people he encounters in "Sheriff Radcliff's Hotel" are victims of society who provide him with little more than interesting stories. The article is professionally written; his reporter's eye misses little. But the drama, the anger, and especially the sense of commitment that infuses "War in Paterson" is largely lacking.

"War in Paterson" was Reed's most mature and brilliant piece of reporting to date. He had unknowingly readied himself to write it by wandering about New York learning to use all his senses to understand his experiences. Yet it was above all Reed's identification with the cause of the striking workers that made this article great. He was always at his best when he wrote from first-hand experience. Paterson was a training ground for his imminent Mexican adventure.

Insurgent Mexico

Reed's *Metropolitan* and *Masses* articles on the Mexican Revolution made him one of the most celebrated young journalists in America. His considerable fame was only enhanced by the publication in July 1914 of *Insurgent Mexico* by D. Appleton and Company. The book, which includes nearly everything of importance that he had written about Mexico, adds definition and cohesion to his remarkable experiences there.[4] Yet it was Reed the poet rather than the journalist who rearranged the articles, provided new material, and even altered the sequence of events to impose continuity, drama, and order on the revolutionary turmoil he had witnessed.

From the opening chapter it is obvious that *Insurgent Mexico* is as much about Reed as it is about a revolution. Even while describing the courage, determination, and resiliency of a population battered by violent social forces, Reed the poet, the journalist, and the radical is never far from the story himself. Although he admitted in his autobiographical essay "Almost Thirty" that in Mexico he was afraid of "death, of mutilation, of a strange land and strange people whose speech and thought I did not know," once there he enjoyed one of the most satisfying and creative periods of his life. "I made good with these wild fighting men," he concluded, "and with myself. I love them and I loved the life. I found myself again. I wrote better than I have ever written" (143).

In a brief opening chapter, "On the Border," Reed sets the tone for *Insurgent Mexico* by describing his activities in the little Texas town of Presidio, which lies across the Rio Grande River from Ojinaja, Mexico. There the remnants of a defeated federal army awaited the arrival of the triumphant Villastas, about to gain control of all northern Mexico. Not content to observe the revolution from across the border or to rely on rumors that swirled like dust in this Texas town, Reed wrote the commanding general in Ojinaja seeking an interview. General Pascual Orozco, another federal commander, intercepted his letter and promised to kill Reed if he tried to enter Mexico. Unafraid, Reed waded across the Rio Grande, wandered about Ojinaja for several hours, and finally got the interview he wanted. The reader thereby learns from the outset how Reed plans to study the revolution. *Insurgent Mexico* is an extraordinary account in which the author and the events he describes are inextricably tied.

Most of *Insurgent Mexico* is the story of Reed's adventures and his impressions of the four months he traveled across the northern Mexican states of Chihuahua and Durango. He vividly recalls riding with a contingent of Villastas, La Tropa, earning their friendship while enduring their hardship. When a number of these mounted irregulars are overrun by enemy soldiers, he brilliantly narrates his own desperate flight across the desert. Pancho Villa is the key to Reed's understanding of the revolution. At this time, he was not yet well known to the outside world. Reed describes his spontaneity, impetuosity, cruelty, military brilliance, and close identity with his peon followers. He then contrasts this romantic military figure with the titular head of the Constitutionalists, Venustiano Carranza. Supposedly, Villa and Carranza had similar goals. But Reed found Carranza to be inactive, rather dull, and aloof from the cause he was leading. In the last third of the book Reed describes going into battle with the Villastas as they moved towards the important rail center of Torreón in southern Coahuila. A concluding section, "Mexican Nights," examines the rhythm of life in two little mountain towns in northern Durango which seem to reflect the kind of symbiotic existence that he believes the Villastas were attempting to bring to all of Mexico.

One of the earliest reviewers of *Insurgent Mexico* observed that reading the book was like viewing a rapid succession of snapshots.[5] Indeed, Reed's approach was largely descriptive, impressionistic, and picaresque. Much like his article on the Paterson strike, this longer work does not purport to be objective. Reed provides virtually no information about the origins of the revolution nor does he search for a socioeconomic explanation of the turmoil. Instead, he describes

scenes, events, and personalities just as he reacted to them. The end
result is an episodic work of dramatic freshness.

When Reed arrived in Mexico, he may have been aware that the
legendary Richard Harding Davis was covering the revolution for
a rival paper. Or he may have felt a lingering sense of guilt over
the failure of the Paterson Pageant. Whatever his reason, Reed felt
compelled to prove himself time and time again. This need to show
his courage may have been part of what Robert Rosenstone describes
as a kind of initiation process whereby the poet became a man.[6]
Reed in fact hinted at this in his autobiographical essay ("Almost
Thirty" 143). Whether he was riding with La Tropa, battling with
Villa's troops, or simply experiencing the day-to-day events of the
revolution, Reed faithfully reported on its progress and on how he
weathered the challenges it posed personally to him.

One excellent example of Reed's reporting as a participant is an
escapade that began when he borrowed a horse from La Tropa. Up
to this point, a stagecoach had been his only means of transportation.
When he joined the other mounted *compañeros* they greeted him
excitedly. The column's captain challenged him to prove his manhood by drinking an entire bottle of sotol—a fiery Mexican alcohol.
" 'It's too much,' I laughed. 'Drink it,' yelled the chorus as the
tropa crowded up to see. I drank it. A howl of laughter and applause
went up" (35–36). Several days after the sotol incident, when there
was no time to build a fire, Reed wrote that the tropa killed a steer
and "we ripped the meat from the carcass and ate it raw" (45). The
author has now joined together with his subjects to become "we."
Reed's acceptance by La Tropa seems to be complete. They ask him
to share their smoky sleeping quarters, filled with fetid breath and
fleas. Oblivious to his surroundings, Reed revels in an authentic
war experience. As he rolls into his blanket he happily notes: "I
slept better than I had before in Mexico" (43).

While visiting a column of La Tropa defending a strategic mountain pass from the enemy, Reed experienced battle for the first time.
In fact, he was lucky to escape unharmed. Staying in a hacienda
several miles from the pass, he woke up one morning to the news
that the enemy had broken through. Chaos followed as officers
shouted orders and friends rode off to stop the enemy advance. No
one seemed to know precisely what was happening. Reed only began
to understand the rebels' desperate situation when a retreating trooper
appeared with half his jaw shot away. A short time later, having

no horse of his own, Reed was running for his life through the chaparral. His masterful description of this flight is strikingly crisp: "I ran. I wondered what time it was. I wasn't very frightened. Everything still was so unreal, like a page out of Richard Harding Davis. It just seemed to me that if I didn't get away I wouldn't be doing my job well. I kept thinking to myself: 'Well, this is certainly an experience. I'm going to have something to write about' " (88).

Some weeks later as the Villastas tried to capture the heavily defended town of Gómez Palacio, which blocked their way to Torreón, Reed experienced firsthand the horrors of a prolonged siege. Death, mutilation, exhaustion, boredom, and courage seemed mixed together in confusing abundance. Lacking sleep, begging food like other soldiers, and risking his life to get close to the fighting, he continued to prove his manhood. After the federalist defenders of Gómez Palacio poisoned the irrigation ditches surrounding the town, Reed, like many others, drank the water. He describes his own agony briefly, almost as an afterthought: "After I had rolled upon the ground in my blankets, terrible cramps suddenly wretched me, and I crawled out away into the brush and didn't have the strength to crawl back. In fact, until gray dawn, I 'rolled very sick on the ground' " (236). With so much death and suffering all around him, he seems indifferent to his own painful poisoning. It is only an expected consequence of war. By suffering like other soldiers, Reed had shown his ability to face the challenge of battle. He had again proven, at least to himself, that he deserved to be with the Villastas.

It is impossible to know how truthful are Reed's accounts of the revolution. In the articles that became *Insurgent Mexico,* he mixed fact with fantasy, the real with the imagined. In "Almost Thirty," and in the early portions of *Insurgent Mexico,* he comments on his poor Spanish, yet reproduces entire conversations that were carried on in the heat of battle. There is no doubt that journalistic accuracy often gave way to Reed's poetic imagination. But this is precisely how Reed intended to write. He never planned just to report on events in Mexico. Instead, Reed hoped to capture the mood of the revolution, the feel for battle, and to learn of the aspirations of the people and their cruelties. He sought to understand a country torn by social strife. Certainly the essence of the revolution transcended the mere recording of events. Reed brilliantly captured its uniqueness in his own impressionistic reporting style.

Much of Reed's imagination crept into his writing as he prepared his articles for publication. One example relates to his journey towards rebel forces converging on Torreón. Reed claims that he was joined by a Mexican friend who at first had wanted to kill him. In fact, his notebooks show that he traveled south with the insensitive American, Mac, whom he later described in a short story for the *Masses*.[7] Here Reed simply employed a little literary license for the purpose of enhancing his story. How much more exciting it was to approach a major battle of the revolution with a Villasta at his side rather than a narrow-minded drifter.

Reed even changed his description of his first meeting with Lieutenant Antonio Montoya, the friend who allegedly joined him on the way to Torreón, for dramatic purposes. According to his notebooks, he, Mac, and Montoya, a man who had shot to death forty-five federalist prisoners, met and drank together in a Chihuahua City bar. The three men later gathered in Reed's room. There Montoya so covetously admired Reed's wristwatch that he gave it to him.[8] In Reed's literary version of the incident, Montoya came to Reed's room alone intending to kill the "gringo." But the soldier changed his mind when Reed gave him the watch. Thus in the fictional account, Reed made the watch a kind of deus ex machina that saved his life. One other deliberate departure from reality that can be found in *Insurgent Mexico* is the chronology of his visit to the little Durango mountain villages. While the visit actually occurred *before* he joined La Tropa, Reed discussed it at the end of the book. In this way he could use the visit as a kind of dramatic coda suggesting a way of life he believed would emerge from the turmoil of the revolution.

Reed reported one part of the story of the Mexican revolution quite accurately—his own love for the country, the people, and their cause. He was, for example, fascinated by the harsh terrain that he crossed with La Tropa: "We rode in a silent, enchanted land, that seemed some kingdom under the sea. All around were great cactuses colored red, blue, purple, yellow, as coral is on the ocean bed. Behind us, to the west, the coach rolled along in a glory of dust like Elijah's chariot. . . . Eastward, under a sky already darkening to stars, were the rumpled mountains behind which lay La Cadena, the advance post of the Maderista army. It was a land to love—this Mexico—a land to fight for" (57).

As for the Mexican people themselves, Reed loved their spontaneity, generosity, resilience, communal inclinations, courage, unwavering love of life, and, perhaps most important of all, their willingness to accept as one of their own this young gringo from the North. Even with his sketchy Spanish, Reed never felt a stranger. Soon after catching up with La Tropa, for example, he became good friends with two of the troopers. Captain Longions Guereca, although roughly Reed's age, was already a seasoned veteran of the revolution. When the other troopers could not understand why Reed refused to fight, Guereca explained that Reed was a reporter, not a soldier. He also made it clear that their friendship was a lasting one: "We shall sleep in the same blankets, and always be together. And when we get to the Cadena I shall take you to my home, and my father shall make you my brother. . . . I will show you the lost gold mines of the Spaniards. . . . We'll work them together, eh? . . . We'll be rich, eh?" (52).

Twenty-year-old Luis Martinez was the other soldier Reed knew well. Like Reed, he had never been in battle. Both men, uncertain about the future, discussed it at length. Often they sat together late into the night "talking about the world, our girls, and what we were going to be and do when we really got at it" (67). When Reed later wrote about the rout of La Tropa at La Cadena, he was not just a journalist reporting on a revolutionary skirmish. Rather, he had now become a *compadre* who had seen his friends ride off to their deaths. Guereca had galloped off promising to look for Spanish mines when he returned. Martinez followed, "shouting to me with a grin that he felt scared to death" (83). After his own escape through the desert, Reed felt no euphoria over his first experience in battle. Instead a sense of grief about so many "useless deaths in such a petty fight," overwhelmed him (98). His account of the rout at La Cadena could only have been written by someone who had been there himself and suffered his own personal loss.

Many of the qualities that Reed most admired in his La Tropa friends he found in the rebel leader of the north—Pancho Villa. With a touch of hyperbole, he called him Robin Hood and likened his military skills to Napoleon's. Still mistrustful of the middle classes, Reed believed that Villa, because of his own humble origins, best sensed the needs of the peasants. Villa understood intuitively that sweeping land reform would be necessary for lasting social change. Given Reed's admiration for Villa, it is not surprising that he shrugged off persistent rumors about Villa's cruelty. Reed argued that the rebel leader saw little difference between civilized and

uncivilized methods of war. From his perspective they were essentially the same. No doubt Reed's great attraction for Villa stemmed
from the ex-bandit's obvious affection for him. Villa treated the
young reporter with a kind of amused tolerance, nicknaming him
chatito (pug nose), chiding him for pressing Villa on his ambition
to be president, or even stopping to speak to him in the midst of
a battle. In an ill-defined way Villa also seemed to represent a part
of the revolution with which Reed identified closely. This can be
seen most clearly in an episode where Reed asked some rebel soldiers
why they were fighting. The answers were, as expected, varied.
Several mentioned land reform, others the love of excitement, and
at least one claimed that it was better to fight than to work in the
mines. But one trooper fighting for "libertad" captured Reed's
imagination.

"What do you mean by *libertad?*"
"Libertad is when I can do what I want!"
"But suppose it hurts somebody else?"
He shot back at me Benito Juarez' great sentence:
"Peace is the respect for the rights of others!" (40)

For Reed, living as one wanted while respecting the rights of others
was a principle that would work as well in the Village as in Mexico.
This was the kind of radicalism that most appealed to him at this
time in his life.

    Reed concludes *Insurgent Mexico* on a tranquil note. In the final
chapter he describes a visit to a mountain village in northern Durango where he sees *Los Pastores,* one of the miracle plays traditionally
presented on feast days. Such plays were as much a part of Mexican
village life as the mud walls of the houses. Each performance was
a social gathering in itself, attended by entire families. Reed was
fascinated by the audience participation in the play—villagers loudly
expressed their views on the traditional moral issues by shouting to
the actors and arguing with one another as they related the universal
themes to their own lives. These ancient plays with their good-
natured, vocal audiences reflected for Reed much that he had grown
to love about the country, especially the vitality and symbiosis of
Mexican village life. He hoped that the revolution would reshape
all of Mexico in this image. But at the time he completed *Insurgent
Mexico,* Reed did not know what the outcome of the revolution

would be. Nevertheless, like the Villastas with whom he had ridden, Reed loved the land and felt it was well worth fighting for.

Reed's mentor Lincoln Steffens found *Insurgent Mexico* an exciting book. His student had used his reporter's skills brilliantly to produce a work that was both imaginative and romantically engaging. Yet it was not without flaws. Steffens wrote to Reed in the fall of 1914 that *Insurgent Mexico* was a youthful book that dealt largely with surface appearances. "Your views on Mexico were not nearly so good as your descriptions and narrative. And that will be so for some years yet. You're not wise, Jack; not yet. But you certainly can see and you certainly can write."[9] *Insurgent Mexico,* as Steffens suggested, was about what a young American had seen and done during his four months in revolutionary Mexico. It is a book of descriptions, impressions, and experiences. While the author writes about Mexico, he also writes about himself. It is also a book in which truth and fiction are sometimes hard to distinguish. Reed altered, embellished, and invented to create a sense of visibility that went beyond mere detail or descriptive analysis. As Gregory Mason, a fellow journalist who was also familiar with Mexico, commented, "it is true that Reed loved a good story too much to spoil one by over-fidelity to scientific exactitude. He liked talk for its own sake. In 1914 I happened to follow Reed from Greenwich Village to Mexico, and back to Greenwich Village. In the Village I heard many exaggerated versions of Reed's belligerent exploits in Chihuahua, and in Chihuahua I heard many exaggerated versions of Reed's amatory exploits in the Village. But they were essentially true in spirit, and that is the point about Reed's writing on Mexico."[10] To be sure, *Insurgent Mexico* enabled Reed to display his considerable talents as a reporter. But far more importantly, the book shows his imaginative skills, his ability to capture so precisely the uniqueness of Mexico, its people and their revolutionary turmoil, while he is also writing about himself. It is this blend of reporting and creating that makes *Insurgent Mexico* an enduring work, as exciting to read today as it was three quarters of a century ago.

Articles 1914–1917

When he returned from Mexico, Reed was an exceedingly popular writer, compared even to the dean of American romantic journalists—Richard Harding Davis. He no longer had to write filler assignments or do endless editorial work. For the first time in his life his writing skills were in demand. As his fame grew, he conducted interviews with Billy Sunday, William Jennings Bryan, and Henry Ford, and also covered the 1916 Democratic and Republican National Conventions. Despite this growing recognition, Reed did not stray from writing on the issues that mattered most to him. His post-Mexico periodical writing focuses on two major topics: the ongoing struggle of American workers for social justice and the First World War. Each of these topics was politically controversial. Each suggests a growing sense of radicalism, tied no doubt to his deepening interest in socialism. But strikes and war were also exciting events within his reach. Given Reed's insatiable appetite for adventure and his professional ambition, it is not surprising that he chose such subjects to write about.

With only a handful of exceptions, most of the three dozen articles that he published during these years appeared in either the *Metropolitan* or the *Masses*. Mildly socialistic and in the muckraking tradition, the *Metropolitan* had become decidedly less radical by 1915. Reed continued to write for the magazine without editorial interference until 1917, when his antiwar views became too embarrassing for the editors. While the *Masses* could not, like the *Metropolitan*, pay Reed for his contributions, its editors always allowed Reed to express his views freely.

Reed's arrest at Paterson in 1913 had prompted little reaction because he still was not well known. But when he went to Colorado in the spring of 1914 to cover the Ludlow Massacre his Mexico reporting had made him a celebrity. His writing from Paterson was also different because he had participated in the event itself. At Ludlow he was more the investigative reporter covering a tragedy that had already occurred. Although "The Colorado War" (*Metropolitan*, July 1914) lacks the vivid, impressionistic, on-the-spot exclusiveness of the Paterson article, it is a well-researched piece in which Reed showed his ability to analyze a complex situation.[11]

After describing the tense atmosphere in the Trinidad mining district that lingered on some ten days after the massacre, he outlined the conditions under which the miners worked and their demands for change, which had led to the strike. He describes the strike itself, the attack on the tent city at Ludlow, and the Wilson administration's sending of troops, ostensibly to maintain peace. Reed argues that the various ethnic groups of workers had learned the meaning of solidarity through their common struggle. But the situation seemed so much more hopeless than it had in Paterson. There, the death of a single striker had become a rallying point for the workers. In Colorado, the bodies of twenty-six men, women, and children at the burned-out camp at Ludlow seemed to confirm how one-sided the class struggle could be.

Some eight months before he and Louise Bryant left for Russia, Jack published another article about a strike ("Industrial Frightfulness in Bayonne," *Metropolitan,* January 1917). Perhaps using the Ludlow piece as a model, he describes a strike of largely Polish immigrant workers in Bayonne, New Jersey, against Rockefeller's Standard Oil Company. Reed made three research trips to this industrial town on the outskirts of New York City. Working with an interpreter, he was able to outline the workers' demands, the nature of the strike, and the violent tactics used against the strikers. What happened at Bayonne symbolized for Reed the growing discontent of all American workers: "In the past few years we have seen the recurrence of a very primitive kind of strike—the strike of the hunger-driven, the desperate, unorganized herd of laborers— the turning of the worm" (12).

From 1914 through early 1917, Reed wrote only six articles that did not in some way relate to industrial workers or to World War I. Four of the six, which resulted from interviews with three well-known public figures, suggest Reed's growing fame. In February 1915, for example, along with artist-illustrator George Bellows, he covered a Philadelphia revival by Billy Sunday ("Back of Billy Sunday," *Metropolitan,* May 1915). Limited to just a few minutes alone with the revivalist by his protective and suspicious wife, Reed and Bellows were more successful in interviewing members of the city's campaign committee, which sponsored the event. Committee members included Philadelphia's more respected ministers and businessmen. In a lengthy interview with Alba B. Johnson, president of the Baldwin Locomotive Works, Reed learned that Johnson and other committeemen hoped that Sunday's kind of revivalism would reduce social unrest and thwart social reform. When asked about Sunday's worth to the city, Johnson replied: "Now Billy Sunday makes people look to the valuation of their own souls; and when a man is looking after his own soul's good, he forgets his selfish desire to become rich" (10). Hypocrite that he was, Johnson nurtured his own soul while he paid low wages to his workers, prevented union organization, and used the black list. Another committee member, a prominent clergyman, had even greater praise for the benefits of the crusade: "The bringing of men to Christ is the first prime fundamental reform; and, of course, after that is accomplished no other reform is necessary" (9).

Reed found most of Sunday's entourage to be as shrewd and calculating as the businessmen who sponsored the revival. He recognized that Sunday was a decent man who could be both sincere and inconsistent. Sunday could attack alcohol while a number of his most important Philadelphia friends were brewers. He could denounce child labor and strikes in the same breath. Ultimately Reed condemned not the man but the system. He showed in his article that the revival had much more to do with social control than with Christian brotherhood.

Within a year of reporting on the Sunday revival, Reed accepted an assignment from *Collier's* to interview another public figure who in many ways, was as blissfully naive—William Jennings Bryan ("Bryan on Tour," *Collier's*, 20 May 1916). Reed joined Bryan on a lecture tour down the Saint Johns river in Florida, several months after he had resigned his cabinet post. Appalled by the triviality of Bryan's mind and the shallowness of his intellectual curiosity, Reed nonetheless paid tribute to his humanitarian instincts and undying commitment to reform. As in his treatment of Sunday, Reed was critical. Yet his evaluation of a man who seemed to be bewildered by events he should have had under control was also kind.

When Reed turned to a sketch of an industrial tycoon, he produced a far more interesting article. Written during wartime, when his radicalism was beginning to take form, this piece, "Industry's Miracle Maker" (*Metropolitan*, October 1916), was surprisingly sympathetic to the pioneering efforts of Henry Ford. If the size of the Ford plant and the "miracle" of the assembly line impressed Reed, he was even more excited over how Ford treated his workers. Such practices as profit sharing and the eight-hour day had made Ford an industrial rebel whom other capitalists feared. Despite his praise for Ford, Reed criticized sexism and found fault with the staff of the company's sociological department for meddling in the lives of the workers. Oddly enough, he was remarkably noncommital about Ford's dislike of unions. This article shows clearly that Reed was not yet tied to a specific ideology, and that he was even willing to consider paternalistic solutions to industrial problems. But Reed was still a Socialist. In a subsequent article for the *Masses,* one which also praised Ford ("Why They Hate Ford," October 1916), he toned down his enthusiasm: "the Ford workmen can get more of the profits and still be slaves—for, after all, their well-being depends upon the benevolent intelligence of one man" (12). Reed may have had his doubts, but he was still attracted to the solitary hero struggling against enormous odds—exactly the kind of figure who appeared so often in his early poems and fiction.

The other subject that attracted Reed's interest during this period was World War I. Unlike his Mexican Revolution pieces, which had been published as a whole in *Insurgent Mexico,* his World War I work never appeared in a single volume. Instead, Reed's *The War in Eastern Europe* consisted only of the articles he wrote about his trip with Boardman Robinson through the Balkans, Russia, and Turkey. Most of his other wartime articles reflect his changing concerns about the conflict. In his earliest work, for example, he tried to analyze the causes of the war. His writing from the fall of 1914 through the spring of 1915 consists of impressions of war-torn Europe and descriptions of the western front. Later articles of 1916 and 1917 argue first against American intervention, and then, after it occurred, angrily portray life in wartime America.

Representative of his analysis of the causes of the war is "The Trader's War" (*Masses,* September 1914), which Reed rushed into print shortly after the fighting started. He argues that the Austro-Serbian conflict was a "mere bagatelle," and found the real cause of the war in the commercial rivalry between the major powers. Reed recognizes the kaiser's autocratic rule and Germany's addiction to blood-and-iron diplomacy. But he also asserts that the war resulted from British and French efforts to exclude Germany from the world's markets. "German capitalists want more profits. English and French capitalists want it all" (16). At this early point Reed saw economic causes at the heart of the conflict.

Even though the editors of the *Metropolitan* were aware of Reed's antiwar views, they still sent him to Europe in the fall of 1914. They hoped he would dramatize World War I as vividly as he had the revolution in Mexico. Such was not to be the case. This was a different kind of conflict with its mechanized and impersonal kinds of destruction. Reed also could not get close to the action—reporters faced too many restrictions—and he failed to develop any real feeling for what was happening. He could never describe as forcefully the

war of the trenches as he had his adventures with the Villastas, or
capture the flavor of conflict as he had during the battle for Gómez
Palacio. He felt as if he were seeing the war secondhand. As a result,
Reed's descriptions of German-occupied France ("German France,"
Metropolitan, March 1915), lack the excitement of most of his Mexican articles. He methodically relates how the Germans made the
French pay the cost of occupation. But, in an effort to be fair, he
claims that the occupying forces accomplished some good in a number of the occupied towns. Nevertheless, the destructive madness
of the war continued to hang over these towns even as civilians and
soldiers tried to return to a normal life.

Far more interesting was Reed's account of his only experience
at the front lines ("In the German Trenches," *Metropolitan,* April
1915). In early January 1915, he, Robert Dunn, and several other
correspondents were allowed to enter the German trenches only a
few miles to the south of Ypres. Guests of the Second Bavarian
Army Corps, they learned about the deadly routine of trench life
during the course of an evening. Reed wrote about the rain, mud,
boredom, and feeble efforts of the soldiers to domesticate their
dugout living quarters. He noted the bodies of French soldiers slowly
sinking into the slime of no-man's-land where they had lain since
the last attack. And finally, he observed that men were being killed
nightly by an enemy that could not be seen in a war that no one
seemed to understand.

After seeing firsthand the horrors of the war, Reed was absolutely
convinced by 1916 that the United States should remain neutral.
His position on neutrality mirrored that of the *Masses,* which devoted
its entire July 1916 issue to an antipreparedness campaign. Reed
argued in his contribution ("At the Throat of the Republic") that
many of those most active in the preparedness movement stood to
gain much from American involvement in the war. Citing congres-
sional statistics, he showed that the owners of steel, copper, nickel,
ship-building, and munitions companies dominated the various preparedness organizations. The working person's real enemy was neither Germany nor Japan, but, as he concluded, that "2% of the
United States who own 60% of the national wealth, that band of
unscrupulous 'patriots' who have already robbed him of all he has,
and are now planning to make a soldier out of him to defend their
loot. We advocate that the workingman prepare himself against that
enemy. This is our Preparedness" (24).

Once the United States entered the war, Reed believed that the conflict would have a hideous impact on American society. "War means an ugly mob madness," he wrote ("Whose War?" *Masses,* April 1917), "crucifying the truth-tellers, choking the artists, sidetracking reforms, revolutions, and the working of social forces" (11). Five months later ("One Solid Month of Liberty," *Masses,* September 1917), he documented the accuracy of his earlier predictions by showing the many ways the state had usurped the freedom of its citizens. The passage of the Espionage Act, the suppression of radical journals, widespread mob violence, racial tensions, systematic attacks on organized labor, and the growth of militarism were all destroying the democratic fabric of the republic. "It is the blackest month for freedom our generation has known" (6), Reed somberly concluded as the United States became more like the war-mad Europe he so detested.

Reed's best antiwar piece did not appear in the *Masses.* Published in the *Seven Arts* (August 1917), "This Unpopular War" contributed, ironically, to that magazine's suppression. Here Reed's analysis was more somber and sophisticated than in earlier efforts. Summarizing his antiwar views from a Marxist perspective, he argued that all classes had contributed to the unthinking nationalism that generated the war. While soldiers on both sides killed one another with surprisingly little rancor, government propaganda and mounting casualty lists aroused civilian hatred. There was also little hope for a negotiated peace once the United States joined the conflict. What Reed most resented, what he made clear in the article itself, was his belief that the war exploited American workers. Even as he wrote, they were being shipped to Europe. There they would kill and be killed for a vague notion of nationalistic democracy trotted out by the government. But Wilsonian democracy had nothing to offer the working classes: "they may or may not realize that political power without economic power makes 'democracy' a hollow sham" (407). More than ever Reed felt that this was not his war, not the workers' war, not America's war. But by the summer of 1917, most of his fellow citizens thought otherwise.

The work that Reed did between his return from Mexico and his departure for Russia is among his best and most mature. His interviews, his accounts of labor struggles, his reports on the war in Western Europe, all show the professional skills of an imaginative, investigative journalist. But this work also bears Reed's special journalistic stamp. Going beyond mere description or entertainment, Reed shaped the material to reflect his radical views. He never intended to be impartial. The world as he saw it through a socialist lens needed to be changed. During these years he offered to the public an advocacy form of journalism. By the time the United States entered the war, the *Masses* became virtually his only sounding board.

The War in Eastern Europe

At first, World War I seemed ready-made for Reed's special talents. To be sure, the canvas was larger and the issues more varied than in Mexico, but this was a drama of such monumental proportions that it seemed to beg his careful scrutiny. Reed sent competent articles to the *Metropolitan*, but they generally lacked the originality of his Mexican pieces. When he returned from the western front in January 1915, he was already thoroughly disillusioned with the war and the massive bureaucracies that appeared to be conducting it. But as a responsible journalist he could not ignore it. And so he eagerly accepted an offer by the *Metropolitan* to join Boardman Robinson on a trip to the eastern front. Reed hoped that the more fluid military situation there would at last enable him to view the war firsthand.

Yet this trip too was something of a disappointment. As he wrote in the preface to *The War in Eastern Europe,* published by Charles Scribner's Sons (1916), Reed and Robinson always seemed to be arriving at major events either too early or too late. With a heavy note of sarcasm, he described the exciting developments they expected to observe but never did: "we were going to see Italy enter the war, Venice destroyed by the Austrians; be in Serbia in time for the last stand of the Serbs; watch Rumania plunge into the conflict; stand by at the fall of Constantinople; accompany the Russian steam-roller to Berlin, and spend a month in the Caucasus reporting barbarically colored battles between Cossacks and Turks."[22]

Yet after seven months on the eastern front, Reed and Robinson had, in fact, experienced a great deal. Instead of battles they had seen the grim aftermath of conflict. Instead of dramatic diplomatic shifts they had observed the routine realities of nations at war or on the brink. "As I look back on it all," Reed confesses, "it seems to me that the most important thing to know about the war is how the different peoples live; their environment, tradition, and the revealing things they do and say" (ix). Here Reed was, perhaps, engaging in rationalization. But it was a mark of his professionalism that he could write so effectively about events so different from what he had expected.

The War in Eastern Europe is one of Reed's more conventional works. Here the author is not, as in *Insurgent Mexico,* as dominant a central character. Nor is he so much a poet as a journalist who reports his impressions of his tour of the eastern front. After he and Robinson arrived in Italy in April 1915, they immediately sailed for Greece where they stayed briefly before traveling on to Serbia. Conditions there graphically showed the hideous impact of war and some of Reed's best writing was on his Serbian tour. Following a short stay in neutral Rumania, the two men managed to enter Russia as the imperial armies were retreating along the eastern front. By using passes and their own guile, they miraculously made their way through Bukovania, Galacia, and eventually to the current Polish town of Cholm, where they were arrested and detained in a tiny hotel room for two weeks. Their success in getting so close to the front had convinced the authorities that they were spies. Eventually they were allowed to go to Petrograd to clarify their status. While there they managed a brief trip to Moscow. When the American ambassador offered no help and the Russians ordered them to leave, Reed and Robinson returned to Rumania. Leaving his companion there, Reed went on to Turkey where he hoped to report on the Dardanelles campaign. But bureaucratic red tape once again kept him from the front. Greatly disappointed, Reed joined Robinson in Bulgaria, a nation that seemed about to enter the war on the side of the Central Powers. When Bulgarian mobilization actually began in mid-September, the two journalists had to leave quickly because of Robinson's British passport. Eventually they made their way back to Greece via Serbia and sailed for home. Both men described their Odyssean travels, Reed producing a number of articles and Robinson several sketches. These pieces along with Robinson's art work and additional notes kept by Reed created *The War in Eastern Europe.*

Reed and Robinson had seen little actual combat in their travels, but much of war's destructiveness. In Serbia, three failed Austrian invasions had ravished the land. As enemy soldiers inflicted typhus on the people, the crowded hospitals and black flags adorning peas-ant houses served as a grim reminder of the relentless miseries of war. In Machva, the two correspondents traveled by rail along "a vast fertile plain, white with fruit orchards in bloom and green with tall grass and new foliage, between uncultivated fields rank with weeds, and past white houses blackened with fire. . . . We passed through little towns where grass grew in the streets and not a single human being lived" (87).

The war on the western front had seemed so much more mechanized and antiseptic than the kind of war Reed observed in the Balkans. Skeptical as ever about stories of atrocities, Reed could verify Serbian accounts. He heard stories of civilians being burned alive and of whole villages being destroyed. Yet the closest he came to hell was on a battlefield on Goutchevo Mountain near the Serbian-Austro-Hungarian border. There in the winter of 1914–15, Austrian and Serbian troops, entrenched at times no more than twenty yards apart, had engaged in combat for nearly two months. "The ground between was humped into irregular piles of earth. Looking closer, we saw a ghastly thing: from these little mounds protruded pieces of uniform, skulls with draggled hair, upon which shreds of flesh still hung; white bones with rotting hands at the end, bloody bones sticking from boots such as the soldiers wear." In the German trenches, death had seemed as unreal as the distant enemy. But here "we walked on the dead, so thick were they—sometimes our feet sank through into the pits of rotting flesh, crunching bones. Little holes opened suddenly, leading deep down and swarming with gray maggots. Most of the bodies were covered only with a film of earth, partly washed away by the rain—many were not buried at all" (97–98).

If the sight of rotting corpses mutilated by combat and neglect brought Reed to the edge of despair, so did the seeming acceptance of war as a way of life. He recounted, for example, the boasting of a lieutenant in the Serbian army: "We Serbians know that all that is needed is the willingness to die—and the war would soon be over . . . !" (49). Reed also remembered a Russian captain's remark on how long he thought the war would last: "What do we care how long it lasts? . . . What do we care—so long as England gives money and the earth gives men?" (117).

While Reed traveled for seven months through the Balkans, Russia, and Turkey, he never felt the need, as he had in Mexico, to prove himself or to test his manhood. To be sure, the dangers were as great. On the eastern front, he dodged bullets, was arrested several times, and always faced the threat of typhus. Yet as he described his adventures in Europe, Reed this time followed a conventional course. He was not a youth testing his courage, but rather a journalist in pursuit of a story. And this time he remained detached from the events he observed and reported on.

Because Reed could muster no sense of commitment to his World War I experience, his account of the war, as compared to *Insurgent Mexico,* seems oddly impersonal. *The War in Eastern Europe* has little to say about camaraderie or newly found friendships, although Reed did find much to admire in the people he met. He noted, for example, the generous hospitality of the Serbians, Russians, and Bulgarians despite their adversity. He also praised the social equality of the Serbians and Bulgarians. He found the joy and spontaneity of the suffering Serbs to be reminiscent of Mexico. Yet he could not identify with a people and a cause. This war was too nationalistic. In this war, all sides had territorial ambitions that seemed to make the death and devastation meaningless. How else, he asked, would the Serbs show so little bitterness? They "seemed to think that the smashing Austrian defeat revenged them for all those black enormities, for the murder of their brothers, for the bringing of typhus" (90). And how else could a Russian officer smugly claim that the peasants believed they were fighting Germany to rid themselves of "poverty and oppression?" (146).

Despite Reed's detachment from the events he recorded, he was still fascinated by life in Serbia and Bulgaria. The rugged Serbian landscape, the independent peasant populations of both countries, and the endurance of the people all impressed him. But Russia intrigued him most. Like Mexico, it was a land of contradictions. Reed noted an inept government that sent soldiers into battle without weapons, a bureaucracy as corrupt as it was inefficient. He commented on a huge secret police, on a tsar whose inner circle thrived on decadence and intrigue. The Russian social system relegated Jews to a deplorable state while an entrenched aristocracy desperately clung to its own privileged position. As for the military, Reed incredulously observed a general staff pursuing a strategy bent on the slaughter of its own troops, and an officer class contemptuous of the peasant soldiers it led. But this was the dark side of Russia. Reed saw beyond it to an anarchistic individualism and joyous spontaneity, which appealed strongly to his romantic nature. He liked the closeness the Russian people felt for their land with its vast plains, immense forests, mighty rivers, and demanding climate. The summer sun never seemed to set as days and nights became one. No one lived by a conventional schedule. Visiting, eating, sleeping, or even the departure of a train occurred at no particular time. After one nearly endless banquet, the exhausted Reed and Robinson learned that "sleep is a ridiculous way to pass the night" (120). Garrulous, hospitable, and inquisitive Russians seemed to be forever discussing their souls, the war, or their country's future over tea and cigarettes. "Almost any conversation might have been taken from the pages of a Dostoievsky novel," Reed recalled. "The Russians get drunk on their talk; voices ring, eyes flash, they are exalted with a passion of self-revelation" (206–7). Russia was a country to be loved and pitied. Neither Reed nor Robinson could figure out why the Russian people tolerated a government so corrupt. From his own experiences Reed could only wonder: "Is there a powerful and destructive fire working in the bowels of Russia, or is it quenched?" (232). He would find an answer much sooner than he expected.

The War in Eastern Europe received generally favorable reviews. One writer hit on the essence of the book by commenting on the "wealth of contrasting material" Reed had gathered.[13] This was no Insurgent Mexico that blended fact with artistic imagination. As Rosenstone suggests, The War in Eastern Europe "is a work that conforms to the contours of experience rather than art."[14] Yet Reed could not help but improvise a little. No great linguist, he provided the English translation for conversations that had taken place in languages as diverse as Bulgarian and Turkish. But accurate reporting was never Reed's strength. He was always more interested in capturing the ambience of a scene, depending on his own sense of the dramatic, on his ability to identify the key parts of a conversation. Yet the war in Eastern Europe was still a far cry from the Mexican Revolution. In Europe the war combined so much nonsense and horror that Reed had little trouble distancing himself from the events he reported on. He never lost the openness and friendliness that made him so effective a reporter in Mexico. But the author of The War in Eastern Europe was no eager participant in the conflict. Instead, he was a professional with all the requisite skills for his trade: a keen eye and ear, excellent descriptive abilities, the audacity to challenge bureaucratic restrictions, a sense of adventure, an engaging personality, and, above all, a genuine love for what he is doing.

Despite Reed's impressive reportorial skills, he did not produce a great book. *The War in Eastern Europe* lacks the essential ingredients that can be found in his best work. Only when Reed identified with the cause he was reporting on did he write with the dramatic vitality and creative flare that informed his best work.

Signed Newspaper Articles

Whether the finished product was a book, an article, a short story, or a poem, Reed most enjoyed using his creativity to interpret and embellish events rather than just report them. Facts were important, of course, and Reed was good at uncovering them. But his poetic sensibilities took him far beyond conventional journalism. Consequently, he sometimes enlarged personalities, magnified descriptions, or simplified conversations to convey how a person or situation first appeared to him. Reed may have been known as a journalist, but he never saw himself as one. When he worked for a newspaper he did it for money or for a chance to see a war or a revolution. Most of his signed articles were written during a short period in 1917 when his strong antiwar views closed all other outlets for publication. Nearly all his other news pieces were accounts from Mexico, Europe, or revolutionary Russia. While Reed's newspaper work is quite competent, he never viewed it as anything other than a temporary means to an end.

Reed's first working arrangement with a newspaper came shortly before he left for Mexico. Hoping to supplement his income from the *Metropolitan,* he agreed to send additional stories to the New York *World.* But Reed did not take this extra assignment very seriously. Toward the end of his Mexican stay he finally sent a brief sketch of Pancho Villa to the *World,* which appeared in its edition of 1 March 1914. A few weeks later while he was preparing to leave Mexico, he evaded Villa's censors by sending the *World* an account (25 March 1914) of the fall of Torreón to the Villastas. On 29 and 31 March he sent two other wires claiming that fighting in Torreón continued. Then on 1 April he again reported that Villa had captured the city. Reed had, in fact, created the confusion by reporting the fall of Torreón a week early. Never a stickler for accuracy, he continued to report on the fighting as he journeyed to Texas, relying on his imagination and the fighting he actually had seen.[15] Apparently, Reed had little enthusiasm for the work he did for the *World.*

It was almost an afterthought, halfheartedly done, for the purpose
of earning a little extra money.

A more substantial piece of work on Mexico was an article that
Reed published in the *New York Times* (27 April 1914), in which
he attempted to explain the causes of the Mexican Revolution.
Intended to head off American intervention, the article was later
issued as a pamphlet entitled *The Causes behind Mexico's Revolution*
by the American Association for International Conciliation (New
York: June 1914). Reed argued that the vast majority of the Mexican
people were primarily interested in land reform, and not simply the
constitutional changes begun by Madero and continued by Carranza.
Only Zapata and Villa supported the economic changes wanted by
the masses, and this is why they were so feared in the United States.
Arguing that American intervention would be catastrophic, Reed
pleaded with his fellow citizens to accept both the economic and
political goals of the Mexican Revolution.

Reed's longest stint as a newspaper reporter was the two and one-
half months he worked as a feature writer for the *New York Mail*.
He did not know that a German syndicate had bought the paper a
year earlier.[16] His work for the *Mail* was quite satisfying. It enabled
him to wander once again throughout the city he had grown to
love. Whether interviewing a boxing champion, describing an execution at Sing Sing prison, or analyzing the demands of revolutionary sailors aboard an unnamed Russian cruiser, he never seemed
at a loss for new material. Although he dealt largely with local
issues, on occasion his anger about the war crept into his reporting.
While watching the merrymakers at a Village fund-raiser for Red
Cross and Allied war relief, he thought about America's ignorance
of the realities of war. Only when war-injured cripples began filling
the cities would Americans learn what Europeans already knew (13
June). Reed also agreed with the *Mail*'s position that many prowar
Americans hoped to profit from the conflict. He wrote several articles
supporting the paper's demand for a 50 percent tax on excess war
profits (13–16, 18–19, 21–23, 25 June).

In all his newspaper work, Reed showed an ability to find worthwhile material and to present it competently. But there is little
spark to these purely journalistic pieces. Missing from most of them
is the conviction and vitality of his best work. In large part, a
newspaper's format put constraints on his special skills. His romantic
temperament and impressionistic reporting style was simply not

appropriate. The qualities that made Reed unique could only surface in other forms of writing.

Drama

If Reed wrote newspaper articles for money, he dabbled in drama for the pure love of it. Whether writing plays for his parents, composing skits at Harvard, directing the Paterson Pageant, describing the miracle plays in Mexico, or working, writing, and acting for the Provincetown Players, he was attracted to the excitement and frantic activity of stage productions. He never saw himself as a serious dramatist, but still enjoyed writing and occasionally acting in plays. In the summer of 1916, for example, he hastily wrote a one-act drama, *The Eternal Quadrangle: A Farce Adapted from the Weiner-schnitzler,* to meet the production needs of the Provincetown Players. Lampooning love and marriage in Shavian fashion, the play was briefly performed by the Players. Reed wisely never tried to get it published.[17] Having more confidence in his only three-act play, *Enter Dibble,* he tried but failed to sell it. This somewhat autobiographical drama was about a Harvard graudate who revolted against his privileged background by becoming a common laborer. Stilted and lacking in dramatic impact, the play was primarily a vehicle for Reed to show his antipathy to the middle class.[18]

Reed eventually published four plays. All were one act in length and all were performed. His first post-Harvard dramatic success was *Everymagazine: An Immorality Play,* which he wrote and directed in 1913 for the literary Dutch Treat Club's annual dinner show at Delmonico's.[19] Reed had been elected to the club soon after coming to New York in 1911. He collaborated on the play with Bill Daly, an editor at *Everybody's,* a magazine with a muckraking past. Daly composed the score and Reed the lyrics. Later they decided to have the play privately printed. Similar in presentation to the skits that Reed wrote and directed at Harvard and in mood to *The Day in Bohemia,* this lampoon playfully satirizes the pretensions and policies of the country's leading magazines. Reed ridicules their patronizing editorial policies, devotion to advertising, and pandering to popular tastes. He singles out older magazines like *Century, Scribner's* and *Harper's* for their entrenched pomposity:

> And tho' Congress does not heed me
> And the Public does not read me
> I'm convinced the people need me
> From the Hudson to the coast.

Reformist magazines such as *Outlook* were only interested in change
if it were popular: "I'm a moderate Reformer / Just because Reform's
the thing." While the *American,* for which Reed worked, was best
known for its integration of advertising with fiction:

> Are you next to reading matter, Are you next
> Do you know the way to brighten up your text
> Stick an ad of Bass's ale
> In the middle of a tale
> Or anything at all that isn't sexed.

The play concludes with the magazines weakly maintaining their
integrity despite an unsettling rumor:

> A silly tale I've heard
> That round the town is flying
> That every monthly organ
> Is owned by J.P. Morgan
> Now isn't that absurd
> Somebody must be lying
> It must not be inferr'd
> That wealth is what we're after
> We greet that gibe absurd
> With supercilious laughter

Because *Everymagazine* was light and in fun, Reed could ridicule
real people and policies. At other times his criticisms were much
sharper and less circumspect. But here he was still poking fun at
that segment of the literary world to which he himself belonged.

In 1913, the *Masses* published a shorter play—*Moondown* (September 1913). The Washington Square Players finally performed it
in 1916 after Reed had become a celebrity. Set in a single room in
a New York boardinghouse, the play's only two characters are roommates who show conflicting attitudes towards reality. Mame, in her
early twenties, is a street-wise, cynically realistic factory worker who
uses her physical charms to get better treatment from her boss.

Sylvia, eighteen, is romantic and naive. She awaits the promised return of a poet she has just met that night, and who spoke so beautifully of the moon and stars. Mame knows that he will never come back. She tries to convince Sylvia that romantic dreams do not exist for working girls: "You're nothing to him but material for a poem. He'll sell you to a magazine for seven dollars" (8). Reed understood that writers, in their own way, could exploit people as mercilessly as capitalists.

In 1916, the Provincetown Players performed a somewhat longer play, *Freedom,* at their wharf theater.[20] This work also deals with the activities of poets and intellectuals. Its unnamed characters suggest archetypal human qualities.[21] Three men (Poet, Romancer, Smith), have dug their way into the room of a fourth, a trusty, in their effort to escape from prison. All the action takes place in the trusty's room. Romancer, as it turns out, only wants to escape if he can do it in a daring way while the poet prefers to write about freedom rather than seek it. The trusty, who has spent eighteen years in prison, first plans to join the escape, but fearing the outside world, he decides not to go. Only Smith truly wants to leave. He admonishes the other three: "I'm willing to grant that you have it on me as far as honor, and patriotism, and reputation go, but all I want is Freedom" (311). Yet freedom never comes. His three accomplices prevent his escape and turn him over to the prison guards. The play ends as Smith denies he tried to break out: "There's not a word of truth in it! I was trying to break into a padded cell so I could be free" (313). Just as in Mexico, Reed's brand of radicalism still centered on the freedom of the individual. But he had also seen the IWW in action at Paterson, had ridden with the Villastas, and had contempt for those who sought an abstract liberation. It was not enough for intellectuals to call for change—they must be willing to implement it.

By the time Reed wrote his last play, *The Peace That Passeth Understanding*, he had seen the revolution in Russia. He had also become very bitter about the war, particularly after the Bolsheviks released secret treaties pertaining to Allied territorial promises when they signed the Treaty of Brest-Litovsk. The *Liberator* published the play in March 1919, and the Provincetown Players performed it late in the month. Set in Paris during the peace conference, the play's main characters are the Allied leaders: Wilson, Lloyd George, Clemenceau, Orlando, and the Japanese delegate, Baron Makino.

Wilson is the chief villain. Ingeniously he tells the others that the Fourteen Points is ambiguously worded to insure that the victors will dominate the world. Baron Makino takes issue with the colonial question and the part of the treaty that finds certain people in the world "incapable of self-government" (28). Wilson explains that such people live in "nations with large natural resources and no army or navy" (28). A concerned Clemenceau asks whether the call for an evacuation of all Russian territory refers only to the Germans. Wilson says no. "It stands to reasons that if the Germans withdraw, the Russians might invade Russia. . . ." Lloyd George then adds: "It means that Russia must be evacuated by everyone except foreigners and the Russian nobility" (29). When Reed wrote his last play he was frantically defending the revolution and denouncing foreign intervention. Yet *The Peace That Passeth Understanding* still contains much of the kind of exaggerated humor that he so dearly loved. Funny as he wished the play to be, it also served an important purpose. It enabled Reed to defend the revolution in which he had by then become so engaged.

When Hutchins Hapgood reviewed Reed's activities with the Provincetown Players, he found him lacking both as an actor and a playwright. "Jack was keen about 'ideas'; not interested in any play, or probably in any other literary form, that did not carry a sociological thesis. He attempted to put over some of these ideas and in the attempt lost his quality as a writer, his feeling as a poet."[22] With these words Hapgood was recalling the Reed who had returned from Russia in 1919 fully committed to the revolution. He was not commenting on the playful Village troubadour who wrote *Everymagazine: An Immorality Play* or who shared with Gig Cook the thrill of moving the Provincetown Players to New York. But Hapgood was correct in one respect. Reed was not a great playwright. As with poetry, Reed used drama to test his literary skills, but it was not a literary form to which he was ever fully devoted. His plays are literary period pieces that quickly lost their freshness with the passage of time. Although Reed failed to create great drama, he never lost his interest in the theater, nor did he forget what a successful Paterson Pageant could be. These thoughts about drama and the theater influenced the way he structured his masterpiece on the Russian Revolution.

Chapter Five
The Writer as Activist

Reed's arrival in Petrograd in September 1917, as the Kornilov Affair still simmered in the Russian capital, reminded him of his introduction to revolutionary turmoil nearly four years earlier in Mexico. He also sensed that his period of writer's block had come to an end—here at last were events he could describe with his pen. Reed could barely contain his excitement in a letter to Boardman Robinson: "There is so much dramatic to write that I don't know where to begin—but I'll have a tale to unfold if ever. . . . For color and terror and grandeur this makes Mexico look pale. We hope to go all over Russia sooner or later."[1] During the next few months Reed traveled considerably less than he had hoped because Petrograd remained the center of revolutionary activity. But he was correct in believing that the revolution would be a thrilling subject for his pen. In fact, what he saw in Russia seemed to diminish the import of his Mexican experience. And the events he witnessed changed not only his writing but his life.

When Reed returned to the United States in 1918, he could not start immediately on his Russian book because the State Department kept his papers for several months. Instead, he continued writing the kind of shorter pieces that he had worked on while he was stranded for six weeks in Christiania. But few Americans at this time shared his enthusiasm for Russia—no major magazine would accept his articles. Excited as he was about events in Russia, Reed could share his experiences only with those who heard his lectures or who read radical publications like the *Liberator* or the *Revolutionary Age* that printed his work.

Articles: 1918

Most of what Reed wrote after he returned from Russia was about the revolution or the new Soviet State. Whether deliberate or not, he rarely discussed material that later formed the basis for *Ten Days*. Instead he often looked at events before or after the November

Revolution or pleaded the Bolshevik cause against mounting American opposition. Only occasionally did he write about events in his own country.

In the spring of 1918, for example, he published a two-part article describing his visit the previous fall to the Russian Twelfth Army on the Latvian front ("Red Russia—A Visit to the Russian Army," *Liberator,* April and May 1918), and a description of the Office of Foreign Affairs in the new Soviet state ("Foreign Affairs," *Liberator,* June 1918). An interesting discussion of the Constituent Assembly appeared in November in the *Revolutionary Age* ("The Constituent Assembly in Russia," 30 November 1918). Reed argued that the demise of the assembly marked a watershed in the conflict between the bourgeoisie and the proletariat. Russia was now embarked on a new era. The anti-Bolshevik majority simply reflected "the impotence of the old-time political state as an expression of the will of the majority" (6). Reed also criticized the assembly for its outdated election lists, and asserted that the Russian masses were glad to see it gone. Only the bourgeois newspapers in France, Germany, and America mourned its passing. While Reed's analysis showed his commitment to the revolution, it also emphasized his contempt for the legalistic orientation of the middle class. In "How the Russian Revolution Works" (*Liberator,* August 1918), he impressionistically surveyed the newly emerging Soviet society before and after the fall of the Provisional Government. In discussing religion, he examined the failure of the Russian Orthodox Church to democratize itself. Reflecting, perhaps, his own beliefs as much as anything else, he also stated that a new ideal of internationalism had "replaced the spiritual food provided by the Church to the hungry masses" (22). While such generalizations were largely based on what he saw in Petrograd, Reed seemed unconcerned about applying them to all the Russian people.

Reed wrote other articles during this period not to analyze or to describe but to defend. In the spring of 1918, for example, he supported the Bolshevik control of the press by arguing that many opposition papers had been engaged in counterrevolutionary activities ("A Message to Liberator Readers," *Liberator,* June 1918). Reed claimed that other papers with a "small bourgeois constituency and a large endowment, were put out of business because the newspapers of the proletarian parties, with their enormous public, needed the paper and the printing shops" (25). In July, he branded the Treaty of Brest-Litovsk a dictated peace and suggested that formal recognition of the Bolsheviks would be a blow against the imperialistic Germans ("Recognize Russia," *Liberator,* July 1918). Finally, in two articles written near the end of the year, he attacked Allied intervention in Russia by asserting that German militarism was a greater threat to Allied interests than Russian Bolshevism ("On Intervention in Russia," *Liberator,* November 1918; "They Are Still There," *Revolutionary Age,* 11 December 1918). In each of these articles Reed's pen was a weapon for the revolution. His purpose was not to entertain but to convert.

In view of Reed's preoccupation with Russia, it is not surprising that only four of the more than twenty articles he wrote in 1918 were on an American topic. One of these pieces was a brief outline of the second *Masses* trial, in which he participated (*Liberator,* December 1918). Another described a visit that he and Art Young paid to Eugene Debs on 4 July in his hometown of Terre Haute. Even though Debs was awaiting trial for violating the Espionage Act, Reed in an oddly nostalgic mood found him to be as much a part of the Middle American landscape as frame houses and picket fences. How then could a community like Terre Haute turn against one of its beloved citizens because of his opposition to the war? Reed could empathize with Debs's predicament, but not with his neighbors. Middle Western complacency was such a far cry from the fervent idealism he had seen in Russia. Only Debs's parting words gave him hope for America's future: "Now you tell all the boys everywhere who are making the fight, Gene Debs says he's with you, all the way straight through, *without a flicker!*" ("With Gene Debs on the Fourth," *Liberator,* September 1918, 9).

Reed was in a far more caustic mood in July when he covered the Chicago trial of over a hundred Wobblies who, like Debs, were in court because of their opposition to the war. His report of the trial was filled with anger and his portrait of the judge with bitterness. As he watched the proceedings, memories of the Smolny Institute became clear in his mind. Judge Landis, Reed thought, not the Wobblies, should be on trial for counterrevolution. But that was a scenario for Russia. There the workers had taken control of the state. Here the state still held them under its thumb.

Reed's last article of 1918 is an important one because it reflects his mood at the time and hints at the direction his writing would take. Didactic in tone and little concerned with literary effect,

"Bolshevism in America" (*Revolutionary Age*, 18 December 1918) is important for other reasons as well. In this piece Reed discusses revolution in America rather than in Russia. He affirms his belief that the IWW rather than the Socialist party or any other labor group is the center of American radicalism—a belief that ultimately led to ideological confrontation during his last trip to Russia. Reed also showed that he understood how difficult his task would be, for he emphasized that the "American working class is politically and economically the most uneducated working class in the world" (3). In the months ahead, he would have to educate to initiate change. This explains in part why he helped found the American Communist party. This also explains why he increasingly subordinated his writing to his beliefs, his career to his ideals. Yet even as his political activities demanded more of his time, Reed still considered himself a poet. No better proof of this is his unfinished poem "America 1918."

"America 1918"

Reed began "America 1918" during the last part of his stay in Russia and continued working on it while he waited for State Department clearance in Norway. Never completed, the poem was published only after his death.[2] Whitmanesque in style and nostalgic in tone, "America 1918" suggests the dichotomy of Reed's career as a writer. Even in the midst of a revolution, he had to write poetry. For Reed there was always a tension between his art and his commitments, his writing and his politics. But this particular poem also suggests that no matter how far from home Reed was, America stayed very much on his mind.

"America 1918," which intends to capture the inconsistencies of a dream unfulfilled, is more a passionate remembrance of things past than a condemnation of present failures. In the opening stanzas Reed shows his disenchantment with America's lofty ideals:

> Across the sea my country, my America,
> Girt with steel, hard-glittering with power,
> As a champion, with great voice trumpeting
> High words, "For Liberty . . . Democracy . . ."

> Deep within me something stirs, answers—
> (My country, my America!)

> As if alone in the high and empty night
> She called me—my lost one, my first lover
> I love no more, love no more, no more . . .
>
> (59)

But Reed's rejection of his country is not convincing. After describing the West of his youth and the joys of Harvard, he devotes the rest of the poem to his great love affair with New York. Youthful and cruel in its bewildering variety, the city still remains as "familiar and unforgettable . . . as the face of my mother . . ." (64). Mother, lover, the city was all things to Reed.

As with most of his poems, "America 1918" is derivative and suggests that Reed had yet to discover a poetic voice of his own. In fact, he set the unfinished poem aside to complete *Ten Days* in a rush of creative energy. However much Reed wanted to be a poet, his best work was still his prose. Yet "America 1918" shows with stark emotion Reed's frustration with his country. Curiously, the poem's inconclusive romantic ending offers more hope than despair: "All professions, races, temperaments, philosophies / All history, all possibilities, all romance, / America . . . the world . . . !" (66). This final stanza also reflects Reed's own dilemma—he could not fully achieve his ambitions as a writer while fighting for revolutionary change at home and abroad.

The Sisson Documents

If "America 1918" portrays Reed the poet, *The Sisson Documents,* published in the fall of 1918, shows Reed the revolutionary. In mid-September 1918, under the auspices of the Committee on Public Information, American newspapers began to print a number of documents that had been secured earlier that year by Reed's old nemesis Edgar Sisson. The documents alleged that prominent Bolsheviks, Lenin and Trotsky included, were German agents in the pay of the German general staff. Since the documents had been in American hands for six months before they were released, Reed suspected that they were being used to justify American intervention in the Russian civil war. He also believed they were forgeries. In *The Sisson Documents,* a seventeen-page pamphlet published by the *Liberator,* in 1918, he attacked their spurious claims.

Reed's pamphlet was a weapon to be used against the enemies of the revolution. His prose is workmanlike and to the point rather than expansive and literary. Reed argues that the Provisional Government, as well as the British and French, had all examined the documents and found them to be worthless. He suggests that the papers prove, at best, Sisson's own gullibility. Reed shows in great detail the inconsistencies in chronology, mistakes in identity, and other inaccuracies that together make the documents a fraud.

Recent scholarship shows that Reed's analysis of the Sisson documents was essentially correct.[3] His hurriedly written pamphlet also hints at where his career would take him after he completed *Ten Days*. He would use his writing more and more as a weapon in the class struggle. Poetry, fiction, and other literary forms would be put aside as he defended the revolutionary movement. Yet all of this was yet to occur, for Reed was about to undertake the most creative effort of his career. He was about to put into writing his view of the ten eventful days that changed the history of the world.

Ten Days That Shook the World

One of the most remarkable qualities of *Ten Days That Shook the World* is how effectively it conveys the frantic atmosphere of Petrograd as the Bolsheviks wrested power from the inept Provisional Government. It is a testament to Reed's skill that he could so vividly recreate such an atmosphere more than a year after the events he was describing occurred. Moreover, Reed had to work with a language that he was still in the process of learning.[4] But the book succeeded in part because of Reed's meticulous preparation. Exiled in a room on Sheridan Square in New York City during the last two months of 1918, he surrounded himself with the material that he had so painstakingly collected. Piles of newspapers, personal notes, decrees, posters, proclamations (many of which he himself had torn from walls), and handouts from all the competing factions suggested that he had spent much of his time in Petrograd gathering the artifacts of revolution. He had also saved English and French newspapers, including the valuable *Bulletin de la Presse,* which the French Information Bureau issued daily in Petrograd. This paper published a list of daily events, as well as speeches and comments by the Russian press that were indispensable in helping recreate a revolutionary chronology. He also used some of the material that he had written for the *Liberator* and the *Revolutionary Age* as well as portions of chapters that he had begun nine months earlier while stranded in Christiania. With this massive material at his fingertips, Reed wrote *Ten Days That Shook the World* from beginning to end in a remarkable two-month period of sustained creativity. Consequently, *Ten Days* has more cohesiveness and thematic development than his books on Mexico and Eastern Europe.

The utter seriousness with which Reed undertook this project is reflected in his determination that the November Revolution be understood within its historical context. Unlike his earlier books, more attention is paid to the background of events, especially those that led to the Bolshevik seizure of power. Preceding the first chapter is a section, "Notes and Explanations," in which Reed outlines the ideologies and personalities of the competing parties, describes the various popular organizations, and explains the peculiarities of Russian parliamentary procedures. In a fifty-six-page appendix, he provides additional documentation in the form of speeches, letters, resolutions, and decrees as well as further analysis of controversial events.

"In the struggle my sympathies were not neutral," Reed admits in the preface. "But in telling the story of those great days I have tried to see events with the eye of a conscientious reporter, interested in setting down the truth" (xii). The truth as Reed understood it could be expressed with all the drama and excitement of a play. Fellow radical and playwright John Howard Lawson was the first to note the dramatic structure of *Ten Days*. In his introduction to the 1967 edition by International Publishers, Lawson divides the book, by chapters, into the different parts of a play. While the early chapters serve as prologue, chapters four and five are act one, showing the people as they rise in triumph against the Provisional Government. Act two, which comprises the next three chapters, dramatizes a classic "reversal of fortune" as the counterrevolutionary forces emerge. In the third act, (chapters nine and ten), the people rise again to save the revolution. Finally, an epilogue of what occurred after the ten eventful days comprises the last two chapters.[5]

Reed believed that the workers in Petrograd emerged triumphant largely because they depended only on themselves.[6] He describes how the Bolsheviks faced opposition from the bureaucracy, the army, the diplomatic community, the bourgeoisie, and even the peasants as they tried to govern a divided country. Yet *Ten Days* ends on a jubilant note when a hastily elected Peasants' Congress supports the revolution in late November 1917. Now the industrial workers and peasants are united, symbolically joined in mass support for their own revolution.

From beginning to end, the role of the masses in the revolution thematically dominates *Ten Days*. Unlike his earlier books, Reed does not here occupy center stage. His skills as a war correspondent were well known by the time he arrived in Petrograd and Reed was no longer concerned about what other journalists might be writing. Older, more mature, he did not need to prove his mettle or test his courage. He could go anywhere he wished in Petrograd; he did not have to seek adventure for its own sake. Reed may have stayed out of the story for another reason as well. What was happening in Russia was so important and so collectively motivated that it dwarfed the individual and minimized the role of the reporter as seer.

If Reed's presence is diminished in *Ten Days*, it is still a vital part of the book, lending an aura of authenticity to his account. His description of a meal shared in Smolny Institute personalizes this hub of revolutionary activity: "For two rubles I bought a ticket entitling me to dinner, and stood in line with a thousand others, waiting to get to the long-serving tables, where twenty men and women were ladling from immense cauldrons cabbage soup, hunks of meat and piles of *kasha,* slabs of black bread. Five kopeks paid for tea in a tin cup. From a basket one grabbed a greasy wooden spoon. . . . The benches along the wooden tables were packed with hungry proletarians, wolfing their food, plotting, shouting rough jokes across the room" (33).

As happened in Mexico and Eastern Europe, Reed often confronted great personal danger while covering the Revolution. When visiting the front near Tsarskoye Selo, he was mistaken for a counterrevolutionary and nearly shot. Yet such episodes enabled him to confirm and dramatize events, not dominate them. He wrote *Ten Days* not to account for himself, but to document "the spirit which animated the people, and how the leaders looked, talked, and acted" (preface, xii).

Committed as he was to showing how the people and their leaders seized power, Reed usually accentuated the activities of the former when explaining the direction of the revolution. Yet when he arrived in Petrograd he scarcely understood their objectives. Was the revolution unique or merely a repetition of the Paterson or Ludlow workers struggling valiantly in vain? In an undated fragment pertaining to the revolution, he noted his concern: "The consummation of the Social Revolution may be soon—it may be postponed. This depends almost entirely upon the preparedness of the working class— its understanding of the situation, its readiness to take advantage of it. If the workers are intelligent and determined, the Revolution can be realized now. If they are unable to overcome their traditional habits of thought—above all, if they have not the will to seize power from the debris of a crumbling world—the final victory may be delayed for years."[7]

But by the time he began to write *Ten Days*, the Bolshevik Revolution, still under attack from all sides, had nevertheless succeeded. Any doubts Reed had about the will and determination of the Russian masses had long since disappeared. As he stated so emphatically in the opening pages of *Ten Days*, it "was the masses of the people, workers, soldiers and peasants, which forced every change in the course of the Revolution" (4). Throughout the book Reed never veers from this theme. The masses, for example, saw the March Revolution as only the "first act," and showed time and again their growing discontent with the Provisional Government (2). Although it was the Bolsheviks who ultimately seized power, "they took the crude, simple desires of the workers, soldiers and peasants, and from them built their immediate programme" (5). At times Reed's thesis shapes rather than records events. His erroneous report on how the Central Committee of the Bolsheviks decided to seize power is a case in point. Reed did not attend a secret meeting of the Central Committee on 23 October in an apartment building in Petrograd, and his rendition of what happened there is apocryphal.[8] According to Reed's account, only Lenin and Trotsky called for immediate insurrection. Then, when the committee decided against seizing power at that time, a workingman changed the course of history: " 'I speak for the Petrograd Proletarian,' he said, harshly. 'We are in favor of insurrection. Have it your own way, but I tell you now that if you allow the Soviets to be destroyed, *we're through with you!*' Some soldiers joined him. . . . And after they voted again—insurrection won" (38).

Subsequent accounts of the Bolshevik Revolution document the overwhelming importance of Lenin's unbending will in calling for a seizure of power. But Reed stresses the central role of the people rather than their leaders, insisting that the Bolshevik coup could not have come about without the support of the masses. "If the masses all over Russia had not been ready for insurrection it must have failed. The only reason for Bolshevik success lay in their accomplishing the vast and simple desires of the most profound strata of the people" (292).

Even as Reed analyzes the revolution after the fall of the Provisional Government, he continues to paint the masses in heroic tones. Few of the people whom Reed meets believe that the Bolsheviks will survive. Many of those he interviews give the party three days at most. Only Lenin, Trotsky, and "the Petrograd workers and the simpler soldiers" believe it would be longer (117). It was almost prophetic that three days after the Provisional Government collapsed, when the Bolsheviks were besieged from all sides, Reed witnessed a *levée en masse*. He saw the workers of Petrograd rush towards the city's outskirts to defend their revolution. It was a sight he would never forget:

As we came out into the dark and gloomy day all around the grey horizon factory whistles were blowing, a hoarse and nervous sound, full of foreboding. By tens of thousands the working-people poured out, men and women; by tens of thousands the humming slums belched out their dun and miserable hordes. Red Petrograd was in danger! Cossacks! South and southwest they poured through the shabby streets toward the Moskovsky Gate, men, women, and children, with rifles, picks, spades, rolls of wire, cartridge-belts over their working clothes. . . . Such an immense, spontaneous outpouring of a city never was seen! They rolled along torrent-like, companies of soldiers borne with them, guns, motor-trucks, wagons—the revolutionary proletariat defending with its breast the capital of the Workers' and Peasants' Republic! (181)

Just as it was the masses who hurled themselves before the advancing Cossacks, it was also the workers who usually paid the highest human cost. Reed and Bryant went to Moscow to observe the revolution in that city and to check on the damage done to the Kremlin by the fighting. They watched as hundreds of workers killed in six days of fighting there were buried in the Brotherhood Grave under the Kremlin walls. Standing in the bitter cold as the endless procession of flag-draped coffins passed by, Reed was deeply moved: "Behind the dead came other women—women young and broken, or old, wrinkled women making noises like hurt animals, who tried to follow their sons and husbands into the Brotherhood Grave, and shrieked when compassionate hands restrained them.

The poor love each other so!" (258). Here, as in so much of Reed's work, analysis yields to pure emotion.

While Reed was present at another pivotal event of the revolution, the meeting of the Constituent Assembly on 5 January 1918, he did not deem it important enough to write about. Instead, he concludes *Ten Days* with what he considered a more significant event—the Peasants' Congress and its success in uniting workers and peasants. With the backing of these two groups assured, the November Revolution was in place. The complete story of the revolution would have to be told in future books.

The "masses" Reed referred to in *Ten Days* included the workers, soldiers, sailors, and peasants he had personally seen in action while he wandered about Petrograd in the fall of 1917. This was not merely an artificial term that he trotted out to fit into an ideological schema. As he sat one October evening in the Petrograd Soviet, he listened to an officer arguing for a continuation of the war. " 'The trouble is not with the Government,' he began, 'but with the war . . . and the war must be won before any change—' At this, hoots and ironical cheers. 'These Bolshevik agitators are demagogues!' The hall rocked with laughter. 'Let us for a moment forget the class struggle—' But he got no farther. A voice yelled, 'Don't you wish we could' " (40). Reed could not forget the class struggle either. It was etched permanently in his mind. He had seen so much that was unforgettable during those November days when the masses took control of their destiny. *Ten Days That Shook the World* is his paean to their victory.

While Reed's admiration for the masses was great, he was far too good a reporter to ignore the role of the Bolshevik leaders in the revolution. During one dramatic moment on 9 November, for example, when the fate of the Bolsheviks still hung in the balance, Reed describes a meeting in the Mikhailovsky Riding-School where the lawyer and longtime Bolshevik, N. V. Krylenko, stood on the hood of a vehicle and pleaded for the support of the armored-car troops. Krylenko's presence was critical in swaying the vote, but Reed stresses that the troops ultimately had to decide for themselves whether to support the revolution or not. Reed imagined that what he observed at the riding school would happen everywhere in Russia. He would see "hundreds of thousands of Russian men staring up at speakers all over the vast country, workmen, peasants, soldiers, sailors, trying hard to understand and to choose, thinking so intensely—and deciding so unanimously at the end. So was the Russian Revolution" (163).

Before the November Revolution Reed had interviewed Trotsky, and he often followed this brilliant orator as he crisscrossed the city carrying the message of revolution to the people. Reed was mesmerized by Trotsky's presence and his eloquence. He described the Bolshevik leader as a kind of revolutionary Mephistopheles, alternately cruel, contemptuous, calm, venomous, fiery, indefatigable, but always in control (71, 93, 135, 203). If Trotsky was the passionate hammer in Reed's analysis, Lenin was the logical anvil. Cool, unemotional, Lenin dominated through his convincing logic. But Lenin does not dominate *Ten Days*. While Reed devotes an entire section of *Insurgent Mexico* to Pancho Villa, he describes Lenin in only a single paragraph:

A short, stocky figure with a big head set down in his shoulders, bald and bulging. Little eyes, a snubbish nose, wide, generous mouth, and heavy chin; clean-shaven now, but already beginning to bristle with the well-known beard of his past and future. Dressed in shabby clothes, his trousers much too long for him. Unimpressive, to be the idol of a mob, loved and revered as perhaps few leaders in history have been. A strange popular leader—a leader purely by virtue of intellect; colorless, humorless, uncompromising and detached, without picturesque idiosyncrasies—but with the power of explaining profound ideas in simple terms, of analysing a concrete situation. And combined with shrewdness, the greatest intellectual audacity. (125)

Well aware of Lenin's critical role in the revolution, Reed nevertheless portrayed him as a leader who succeeded because he understood and carried out the will of the masses. Reed never ventured far from his theme that the Bolsheviks could not have succeeded without the soldiers, sailors, and workers who fought for what they believed.

Just as Reed gave the masses a greater role in the revolution than the Bolshevik leaders, he also subtly used descriptive imagery to embellish but not to dominate the revolutionary victory of the Russian people. Recalling Reed's reporting skills some years later, fellow Communist and writer Joseph North argued that "the finest writers of reportage are artists in the fullest sense of the term. They do their editorializing through their imagery."[9] Editorializing was endemic to Reed's writing. But in *Ten Days* his descriptions are sharper, his images more controlled than in earlier books. When he was in New York trying to reconstruct the turbulence of revolutionary Petrograd, images of the French Revolution frequently came to mind. The working-class section of Viborg, for example, seemed similar to Saint Antoine in Paris. The dramatic presence of the Kronstadt sailors in the city on 6 November reminded him of the arrival of troops from Marseilles in July 1792, singing the "Marseillaise." Somewhat later, of course, he understood that the victory against Kerensky and the Cossacks at Pulkovo was much like the French defense of their revolution at Valmy. Reed believed that in the long term the Russian Revolution would be more important than the French. But in *Ten Days* he encouraged his readers to recognize the parallels between the two.

In Reed's account of the growing tensions that led to the Bolshevik seizure of power, the protean atmosphere of Petrograd also plays a salient role. Much as Andrew Bieley did in *St. Petersburg,* his brilliant novel about the 1905 Revolution in Saint Petersburg, Reed treats the city as a major character in the drama. To the most casual observer in the fall of 1917, the long breadlines in the capital told of the terrible misery brought on by the war. But Reed's description of the city shows how it hid such concerns with the schizophrenic gaiety of its nightlife. Like a patient ignoring a fatal illness, life in Petrograd went on as usual. Meanwhile, the social, economic, and political crises intensified. Even as the Winter Palace was about to fall, parts of the city seemed bent on ignoring the danger. In the neighborhood of the Winter Place, "the street-cars had stopped running, few people passed, and there were no lights; but a few blocks away we could see the trams, the crowds, the lighted shop-windows and the electric signs of the moving-picture shows—life going as usual" (83).

Besides his portraits of the city, Reed also used weather conditions to depict the changing revolutionary atmosphere. The bleak Russian autumn seemed to reflect the oncoming demise of the Provisional Government. "September and October are the worst months of the Russian year—especially the Petrograd year. Under dull grey skies, in the shortening days the rain fell drenching, incessant. The mud underfoot was deep," he remembered, "slippery and clinging. . . . Bitter damp winds rushed in from the Gulf of Finland, and the chill fog rolled through the streets" (11). Reed also uses atmospheric conditions to dramatize the fall of the Winter Palace, the triumph of the Bolsheviks, and the uncertainty of what lay ahead on the morning of 8 November: "Although it was six in the morning, night was yet heavy and chill. There was only a faint unearthly pallor stealing over the silent streets, dimming the watch-fires, the shadow of a terrible dawn gray-rising over Russia" (111). In the final chapter of *Ten Days,* as workers and peasants are about to unite, Reed senses the joy that will come as he watches the city happily welcome the first snowstorm. "Everybody was smiling; people ran into the streets, holding out their arms to the soft, falling flakes, laughing. Hidden was all the greyness; only the gold and coloured spires and cupolas, with heightened barbaric splendor, gleamed through the white snow." The transformation was astonishing, as "even the sun came out, pale and watery, at noon. The colds and rheumatism of the rainy months vanished. The life of the city grew gay, and the very Revolution ran swifter" (293).

During the last weeks of the Provisional Government, Reed dashed back and forth between Smolny Institute and the Marinsky Palace where the Council of the Republic, (the so-called Pre-Parliament), was in session. After the Kornilov Affair, a democratic congress had convened in Petrograd in September under the auspices of the All-Russian Central Executive Committee of the All-Russian Congress of Soviets. Hoping to lay the groundwork for permanent democratic government, this congress created the Council of the Republic as a provisional legislative body until the meeting of the Constituent Assembly. Although the Bolsheviks boycotted the Pre-Parliament, this body began meeting on 20 October and continued until the fall of the Provisional Government. It represented one of the critical centers of opposition to the Bolsheviks.

Reed's description reveals his own views of the Pre-Parliament: "There stretched the rows of Bolshevik seats—empty since the first day when they left the Council, carrying with them so much life. As I went down the stairs it seemed to me that in spite of the bitter wrangling, no real voice from the rough world outside could penetrate this high, cold hall" (58). He saw Smolny in quite a different light. This place was a virtual revolutionary beehive from which radiated the dynamism so lacking in the Marinsky. As Bolshevik power spread through the city, the committee rooms at Smolny literally "buzzed and hummed all day and all night" (41). On 6 November, the great meeting hall in Smolny filled with workers and soldiers, creating "a monstrous dun mass, deep-humming in a blue haze of smoke" (69). Finally, on the morning of 7 November, as the Bolsheviks fanned out from Smolny to capture key points in the city, the building seemed to radiate their energetic dedication. Reed completed the often-used metaphor: "Behind us great Smolny, bright with lights, hummed like a gigantic hive" (73). It seemed at long last that history's drones were beginning to control their own destinies. Reed's descriptive imagery records the excitement and enthusiasm that he too felt as he watched the process unfold.

Reed's subjective reporting in *Ten Days* went far beyond his imagery. His stand on the revolution is made clear in the preface—the Bolsheviks are "the only party in Russia with a constructive program" (xi). Reed was no detached journalist when he threw out leaflets from the back of a truck announcing the fall of the Provisional Government. Moreover, as the following incident shows, he never tried to mask the contempt he felt for the enemies of the Bolsheviks. Shortly after the Bolsheviks seized power, the counterrevolutionary forces created a Committee for Salvation to coordinate opposition. On 12 November, a friend of Reed's took him to the secret headquarters of the committee. Instead of exulting at this journalistic coup, he was angered by the committee's activities. His first question made no pretense of impartiality:

"Why," I asked, "do you publish such lies in your newspaper?"

Without taking offence the officer replied, "Yes, I know; but what can we do?" He shrugged. "You must admit that it is necessary for us to create a certain frame of mind in the people. . . ."

The other man interrupted. "This is merely an adventure on the part of the Bolsheviki. They have no intellectuals. . . . The ministries won't work. . . . Russia is not a city, but a whole country. . . . Realising that they can only last a few days, we have decided to come to the aid of the strongest force opposed to them—Kerensky—and help to restore order."

"That is all very well," I said. "But why do you combine with the Cadets?" (211)

In this conversation Reed confronted the two groups he most often ridiculed for opposing the Bolsheviks: intellectuals and the middle class. Many in these two groups were associated with the Cadets—the Constitutional Democrats. Reed believed that neither group, because of its class-blinding myopia, could understand the revolution.

Reed's distrust of middle-class values derived from his writing

career in New York and the years he spent in Greenwich Village.
He had seen nothing in Russia to allay his suspicions. Kerensky
and the moderate Socialists, he argued, had lost the support of the
masses because they aligned themselves too closely with the propertied classes. Not only were the propertied classes opposed to the
social side of the revolution, they were also, in Reed's mind, in-
stinctively antidemocratic. He remembered one evening's experience
dining at the home of a prominent merchant. The guests voted on
their preference for a German or a Bolshevik victory. The tally was
ten to one in favor of Kaiser Wilhelm. Later, when the Bolshevik
uprising began, Reed remembered the street-corner tableaux that
reflected the class conflicts behind the revolution: "On every corner
immense crowds were massed around a core of hot discussion. Pickets
of a dozen soldiers with fixed bayonets lounged at the street-cross-
ings, red-faced old men in rich fur coats shook their fists at them,
smartly-dressed women screamed epithets; the soldiers argued feeb-
ly, with embarrassed grins" (83).

Reed's contempt for the middle class was so deeply ingrained that
he often could not write about its opposition to the Bolsheviks
without being sarcastic. Consider his comparison of the Petrograd
City Duma, where opposition to the Bolsheviks was centered with
the Congress of Soviets at Smolny: "There, great masses of shabby
soldiers, grimy workmen, peasants—poor men, bent and scarred
in the brute struggle for existence; here the Menshevik and Social
Revolutionary leaders . . . the former Socialist Ministers . . .
rubbed shoulders with Cadets like oily Shatsky, sleek Vinaver; with
journalists, students, intellectuals of almost all camps. This Duma
crowd was well-fed, well-dressed; I did not see more than three
proletarians among them all" (120).

It was particularly galling to Reed that Socialists would ally
themselves with the middle classes. But he rationalized their actions
by believing that many who did so were also intellectuals. In earlier
stories and plays Reed had already shown his scorn for the inertia
of intellectuals (*Freedom*) or their tendency to be exploitative in their
art (*Moondown* and "Another Case of Ingratitude"). Once in Russia,
he had found that many intellectuals continued to oppose the revolution largely because it was not developing as they had hoped.
Others resisted the revolution because the intelligentsia did not
support it. In a conversation Reed claimed to have overheard while
he was visiting the revolutionary front at Tsarskoye Selo, he dra-

matized the arrogance and contempt that Russian intellectuals were capable of showing towards the Bolsheviks:

A tall young man with a supercilious expression, dressed in the uniform of a student, was leading the attack.

"You realize, I presume," he said insolently, "that by taking up arms against your brothers you are making yourselves the tools of murderers and traitors?"

"Now Brother," answered the soldier earnestly, "you don't understand. There are two classes, don't you see, the proletariat and the bourgeoisie. We—"

"Oh, I know that silly talk!" broke in the student rudely. "A bunch of ignorant peasants like you hear somebody bawling a few catch-words. You don't understand what they mean. You just echo them like a lot of parrots." The crowd laughed. "I'm a Marxian student. And I tell you that this isn't Socialism you are fighting for. It's just plain pro-German anarchy!" "Oh yes, I know," answered the soldier, with sweat dripping from his brow. "You are an educated man, that is easy to see, and I am only a simple man. But it seems to me—"

As the argument continues, the student becomes even more abusive and condescending:

"And I am opposed to the Bolsheviki, who are destroying our Russia, our free Revolution. Now how do you account for that?"

The soldier scratched his head. "I can't account for it at all," he said, grimacing with the pain of his intellectual processes. "To me it seems perfectly simple—but then, I'm not well educated. It seems like there are only two classes, the proletariat and the bourgeoisie—"

"There you go again with your silly formula!" cried the student.

"—only two classes," went on the soldier, doggedly. "And whoever isn't on one side is on the other. . . ." (186–87).

This particular exchange, as so many others Reed includes in his book, closes with an ellipsis, suggesting a continuation rather than a conclusion of the ideas expressed.[10] In fact, this particular exchange so aptly states Reed's own views that it may reflect poetic license rather than accurate journalism.

Still, in condemning intellectuals as a class, Reed had to explain the intellectuals among the leading Bolsheviks. Lenin, Trotsky, and others in the party were certainly not workers. This problem clearly troubled Reed, for he included teachers, students, and professionals on a list of enemies of bolshevism. At the same time, he also placed on the Soviet side "the rank and file of the workers, the sailors, all the undemoralized soldiers, the landless peasants, and a few—a very few—intellectuals" (244). This kind of analysis is reductionist. Reed is like a guilty child with hand in cookie jar, arguing that he has only taken one or two.

By the time Reed began to write *Ten Days,* American hostility to the new Soviet government was mounting. With lurid tales about Bolshevik excesses already widespread, Reed found himself defending the revolution as much as he described it. For a veteran war correspondent hardened to the horrors of conflict in Mexico, Ludlow, and Serbia, the horror of the Russian Revolution was somewhat muted. Excesses, Reed believed, were part of any social upheaval, especially one as volatile as a revolution. He was also convinced that the Bolshevik Revolution was truly unique and would ultimately benefit working people the world over. In this way he could excuse much of the violence he observed. Reed, in fact, seldom dwells on any particular abuses. Instead he reports them as inevitable incidents in the revolutionary process. For example, he never tries to hide the brutality both sides engaged in immediately after the Bolshevik seizure of power. He also calls a Bolshevik spy system, control of the press, and harsh penalties for counterrevolutionaries necessities of war. Moreover, Reed matter-of-factly reports an incident in which the Bolsheviks tried to stop the looting of wine cellars throughout the city by sending in machine-gun squads to fire into the drunken mobs. None of this suggests that Reed was insensitive to the suffering he saw in Russia, but he dramatized it considerably less than he had in *Insurgent Mexico* or *The War in Eastern Europe.* In *Ten Days,* Reed describes the rise of the masses: everything else in the book is subordinated to that theme. What happened in Russia was so vast and overwhelming that the story could only be told in cosmic terms. "Old Russia was no more;" Reed wrote near the beginning of the chapter devoted to the counterrevolution, "human society flowed molten in primal heat, and from the tossing sea of flame was emerging the class struggle, stark and pitiless—and the fragile, slowly-cooling crust of new planets" (150).

The magnitude and confusion surrounding the revolution also help to explain some of the mistakes Reed made in *Ten Days.* Time, distance, and language hindered his efforts to piece together the flow of events, to connect speakers with speeches, to identify the ideologies and supporters of competing factions while also trying to recreate the tension and excitement of those unforgettable November days. Given the complexity of the revolution and the difficulty of reporting it, it is not surprising that *Ten Days* contains errors of identity, spelling, chronology, authorship, and interpretation.[11]

One of Reed's more glaring errors is his fabricated account of the 23 October meeting of the Bolshevik Central Committee. He also incorrectly reported a story about Lenin. According to *Ten Days,* Lenin attended an historic meeting at Smolny Institute on 3 November, during which he announced that four days hence would be the most propitious time to overthrow the Provisional Government. Reed said he learned this as he sat in the corridor while the highly secret meeting took place, and was informed of what transpired by one of the departing Bolsheviks. But the story cannot be true. Lenin remained hidden in Petrograd until 6 November, and did not arrive at Smolny Institute until around midnight that evening.[12] The speech Reed attributed to him was apocryphal. Were such errors deliberate? Probably not, as Robert Daniels suggests. In the midst of revolutionary turmoil, Reed could easily have confused secondhand verbal reports of Bolshevik meetings.[13]

A more fanciful and less serious distortion was contrived by Reed to protect Vladimir A. Antonov-Ovseenko, Bolshevik commander in chief of the Russian armies, and P. E. Dybenko, the people's commissar for the navy. They had allowed him, Alex Gomberg, and Albert Rhys Williams to go with them to the front on 10 November. Since Lenin had already denied them permission to go, Reed feared that an accurate account of the episode would cause trouble for the two commanders. Williams says that he and his friends rode in a car commandeered by the Bolshevik commandants. In *Ten Days,* Reed claims that he and Williams went by train and that only a comrade, Trusishka, actually reached the front.[14] Reed's description of this episode, distorted as it is, helps to humanize the Bolsheviks and to show the chaotic improvisation that so often occurred in the early days of the revolution. Early in the journey, Dybenko stopped for food, only to find that neither he nor Antonov-Ovseenko had any money to pay for it. Trusishka (one of the Americans) bought it for him. When their car had a flat tire, Antonov-Ovseenko tied to persuade a group of soldiers going to the front to give him their vehicle. Even after he identified himself, the driver replied "I don't care if you're the devil himself. . . . This machine belongs to the First Machine-Gun Regiment, and we're carrying ammunition in it, and you can't have it" (182). The two commandants and their American passengers (in Reed's version, Trusishka) finally approached the front in a battered taxi flying an Italian flag. Then, as they neared the Bolshevik lines, Antonov-Ovseenko wanted to send an order to Smolny for more ammunition, but he had no pencil. Again, one of the Americans (Trusishka) came to the rescue. Experiences such as these gave Reed a useful frame of reference. He could see the revolution in more human terms; he could write about it not as a political abstraction but as a living reality.

While there are mistakes in *Ten Days,* Reed still devoted more care and deliberation to this book than to anything he had done previously. Moreover, he had not intended to compose a journalistic description of the November Revolution. Instead, he wanted to recreate the drama of "one of the most marvelous [adventures] mankind ever embarked upon" (xii). No other world experience equaled that of the Russian masses throwing off centuries of backwardness to control the state. Reed had been a part of this great moment, and to do it justice in his writing, he had to go beyond factual description and political analysis. He had to capture its intrinsic meaning.

To this day, there is much debate about the propriety of journalists participating in events they write about. Donald Pizer, a commentator on the "new journalism" of the sixties and seventies, makes a distinction between the documentary narrative and the documentary narrative as art. The former is concerned primarily with the event as event, or simply with what has happened, while the latter concentrates on the meaning of the event. Pizer suggests, "as in most literary works, verisimilitude is ultimately a means towards an end rather than an end in itself, although the author of documentary narrative may seek to suggest the contrary."[15] In striving for verisimilitude the author is not content to catalogue the chronology of the event, but thematically directs it by selection, emphasis, and interpretation. From Reed's perspective, the November Revolution was much more than a coup d'etat by a highly organized revolutionary minority. It was the historical maturation of the Russian masses. It was their heroic triumph achieved in the face of nearly hopeless odds.

During his first trip to Russia in 1915, Reed had grown to like the Russian people and to admire their stubborn resiliency. When he returned to Russia in 1917, he had been deeply moved by their idealistic determination and unbending courage. His task was to recapture their conflicting emotions, joys, fears, and dreams, which, taken together, constituted the unique meaning of those ten eventful November days. In his approach to the revolution Reed was carrying on a continuing literary tradition. As historian William Stotts suggests, the essence of documentary expression is not simply its capacity to convey information but instead its power to move the reader.[16] While discussing James Agee's 1941 masterpiece, *Let Us Now Praise Famous Men,* Stotts argues that Agee's participation in the lives of the sharecroppers enabled him to view each family member as a unique individual to be liked or disliked, enjoyed or feared. The longer he stayed with the families, the stronger his bond of affection became.[17] Reed had the same experience, first in Mexico and then to a greater extent in Russia. The more closely he identified with the Russian people and their aspirations the easier it was for him to write about them and their revolution. His empathy was not contrived. Reed had shared their feelings and emotions as he wandered through Petrograd and traveled in the countryside. Like Agee, he too loved his literary subjects. Paradoxically, this made his task at once easier and more difficult. A friend, Angelica Balabanoff, believes that it was Reed's love of Russia that helped him overcome his ignorance of the language when he wrote *Ten Days.*[18] This same love enabled him to write *Ten Days* at an incredible pace and also steeled his determination to capture the meaning of the revolution without distorting it or subordinating it to anything else. Consequently, for the first time in his life, Reed wrote a book in which he plays an intrinsic, but not a dominant part.

Reactions and Reviews

When Reed returned to Russia in the fall of 1919, he learned to his delight that Lenin had taken the time to read *Ten Days.* Even more gratifying was Lenin's agreement to write an introduction for the book. This piece first appeared in an American edition in 1922. Although brief, Lenin's remarks were full with praise: "Unreservedly do I recommend it to the workers of the world. Here is a book which I should like to see published in millions of copies and translated into all languages."[19] Just how many workers eventually read *Ten Days* is difficult to say. But in his study of the growth of American communism, Theodore Draper writes that this book converted more people to the Soviet cause than the combined efforts of all other left-wing propaganda.[20] *Ten Days* eventually fell into disfavor in Russia because of the book's many references to Trotsky and few to Stalin. Yet *Ten Days* continued to introduce both workers and nonworkers to the Bolshevik Revolution. Fellow radical Emma Goldman, for one, recalls how it helped her forget prison life when she was serving a sentence for conspiracy to obstruct the draft. "I ceased to be a captive in the Missouri Penitentiary and I felt myself transferred to Russia," she recalled in *Living My Life,* "caught by her fierce storm, swept along by its momentum, and identified with the forces that had brought about the miraculous change. Reed's narrative was unlike anything else I had read about the October Revolution."[21]

Mindful of its errors, scholars today still use and praise *Ten Days*. In his detailed study of the Bolshevik Revolution, Robert Daniels recommends the book for its drama, not its accuracy.[22] British historian A. J. P. Taylor calls *Ten Days* the best account of the Bolshevik Revolution and in many ways the best account of any revolution that he has read.[23] Finally, American diplomat and historian George Kennan criticizes Reed for being "childish and irritating" and notes that he could be "grievously wrong about many things." But Kennan also finds that "Reed's account of the events of that time rises above every other contemporary record for its literary power, its penetration, its command of detail. It will be remembered when all the others are forgotten."[24]

Oddly enough, in view of the hysterical atmosphere of postwar America, *Ten Days* was generally received more favorably than either of Reed's other two books. Of course, there were those who deplored his radicalism almost as much as they disliked the Bolsheviks. The *New York Times* reviewer, for example, argued that Reed had failed to analyze the meaning of the revolution and was the kind of writer who could see social progress emerging only from the barrel of a gun.[25] Another reviewer found in the book all the familiar defects of first-person history. "The narrative is broken into bits, and events and personalities are thrown out of proportion, because the observer is limited . . . in history by the exigencies of transportation, armed guards, and all the other barriers to omnipresence."[26] Such critical comments notwithstanding, reviewers generally praised Reed's descriptive talents, documentation, and ability to recreate the tense atmosphere of revolutionary Petrograd. In one of the most laudatory reviews, fellow Harvard alumnus Harold Stearns noted a difference in *Ten Days* from Reed's other works. "Those who remember Mr. Reed for his fine impressionistic descriptions of the revolution in Mexico will perhaps be taken back at the almost severe quality of this present narrative. With opportunity after opportunity for 'purple patches' Mr. Reed shows a restraint which practically vacuum-cleans the book of any mere rhetorical passages."[27] Stearns and other reviewers also appreciated Reed's frankness in announcing his prejudices. One English reviewer, in fact, even suggested that Reed's subjective stance in writing *Ten Days* was predictable. "His sympathies are obvious, but it is difficult to read the scenes of great popular enthusiasm he describes and to believe that a man could witness them and remain strictly neutral."[28] For Reed remaining neutral had not been difficult, but impossible.

Chapter Six

The Writer as Propagandist

When Reed returned from Russia in 1918, he had, in a sense, already begun to undergo a personality change. Not only was he more serious, but he was altering his personality to conform to his changing political beliefs. The change was even more evident in 1919. At this time he devoted most of his energies to organizing and writing for an American Communist party. "Reed was by character a poet and man of laughter and imagination," his friend Max Eastman later recalled. "He had to change his nature and mode of life as well as dedicate his allegiance."[1]

The changes Eastman noted in Reed's personality are also reflected in much of his writing. By 1919, Reed's work was more serious, didactic, and ideological than during any other period in his life. Whether defending the revolution in Russia or helping to stir one at home, Reed saw himself as the initiator rather than the observer of change. Citations from Marx, which he was then reading, often punctuate arguments in his articles. Theory and history frequently replace personal descriptions and impressions, especially in articles for communist publications. In short, his art took the form of his revolutionary beliefs.

Articles in the *Liberator*

Although Reed resigned from the editorial board of the *Liberator* in August 1918, he never stopped sending articles to the magazine. Stylistically and thematically these articles were not much different from his earlier work. They covered a wide variety of topics, usually offering Reed's personal reflections on events he witnessed in the United States or Russia. Reed still cloaked his anger in humor or satiric description, and often ridiculed through exaggeration. He no doubt tempered his writing because of Eastman's cautious editorial policy and because he realized that not all *Liberator* readers were dedicated Communists. In January 1919, for example, he spoofed the anti-Bolshevik hysteria of so many American newspapers. To counter this pejorative view of bolshevism, he offered his own lighthearted definition. "It is not Anarchism, it is not Vegetarianism, it has no connection either with Free Love or the *New Republic;* in a word it is Applied Socialism, and that is all there is to it" ("Great Bolshevik Conspiracy!" February 1919, 32). In another article he lamented the deaths of the German Spartacists Karl Liebknecht and Rosa Luxemburg and compared their murders to the lynching of Wobbly organizer Frank Little in Montana ("Liebknecht Dead," March 1919). Reed also blamed the destruction of the Spartacist uprising and the murder of Spartacist leaders on the German Social Democrats, whom he labeled the "Kaiser Socialists," for having used imperial troops against the workers (18). And he channeled his anger creatively by eulogizing the two martyred German Communists while attacking the conservative forces in Germany that engineered their deaths.

Reed's attendance at the annual American Federation of Labor convention in Atlantic City led to another article. In a piece appropriately entitled "The Convention of the Dead" (August 1919), he delighted in ridiculing the union's conservatism. Perhaps the conventioneers reminded Reed of the counterrevolutionaries he had seen in the Petrograd City Duma. Here he found little difference between the union's delegates and those of the National Association of Car Manufacturers who were meeting in the same hall. To make matters worse, during the convention, there seemed to be no connection between the needs of the working classes and the activities of the union leadership. It seemed fitting to a satirical Reed that "this Convention should meet in a hall at the end of the pier stretching out to sea. It held itself aloof, not only from the new currents of thought and action flowing through the outside world, but from the labor movement of America" (15). Reed deplored what he believed was the union's business-oriented outlook—an outlook that undermined working-class solidarity. Unlike party theoreticians in Moscow, he later believed that the self-centered elitism of unions like the American Federation of Labor had to be destroyed if revolution was to have a chance in America.

In 1919, Reed continued to write articles in which he defended the Soviet Union by attacking Allied intervention in Russia ("The Latest from Russia," February 1919; "Prinkipo and After," April 1919). But he also began taking a greater interest in affairs at home. "Our Own Black Hundreds" is typical of his analysis of postwar conditions in America (February 1919). In this brief piece he attacked the National Security League, founded in 1914 to lobby for a strong national defense. By 1919, the organization had become superpatriotic, leading other like groups in an assault on aliens and radicals.[2] In Reed's opinion, members of the National Security League understood the nature of the class struggle quite well. They used their organization to shape postwar America in their own conservative, nationalistic image. Reed too wanted to reshape America, but he sought revolutionary, not nationalistic change.

Reed also took an interest in how the war, with so much devastation in its wake, could provide a positive foundation for change. Servicemen had learned to fight for what they wanted. Facing unemployment and little economic opportunity, in postwar America they would confront the realities of the class struggle ("The Blessings of Militarism," May 1919). "They will soon see that it is not we, who champion the working class whenever it asserts its rights, who are their enemies," he predicted, "but those who, having sent the soldiers out to risk their lives for democracy and liberty, have abolished liberty and democracy at home" (30).

In writing for the *Liberator,* Reed never tried to disguise his radicalism. Still, in tone and style his articles were more the work of a radical reporter than a revolutionary. Whether denouncing conditions in postwar America, commenting on international events, or defending the Bolsheviks, he described more than he agitated, explained more than he theorized. Yet predicting and analyzing revolutionary change was a far cry from actively encouraging it. By 1919, Reed thought of himself as a revolutionary—a revolutionary whose writing should be committed to the class struggle. He had brilliantly described the fall of the Provisional Government and the Bolshevik seizure of power in *Ten Days;* now in 1919 he was determined to show through nascent communist publications that a similar process was both possible and necessary in his own country.

Articles in Communist Publications

In writing for the *Revolutionary Age,* and later for the *New York Communist* and the *Voice of Labor,* Reed was appealing to a somewhat different audience than he had in the *Liberator.* In these communist publications, he was writing for other revolutionaries or revolutionaries-to-be among the working class. Even so, a number of these pieces were thematically similiar to those in the *Liberator*. The most interesting are those in which he examined the country's revolutionary potential or theorized about the application of bolshevism to America. He tended to rely more on history and ideology than on imagination, personal observation, or description. These articles were somber, straightforward, polemical, and, for the most part, different from his work to date. Reed was thoughtful rather than brilliant, according to Granville Hicks, who was a party member in the 1930s.[3] The same can be said of the other work Reed did in 1919. His writer's interest had shifted. At the moment he was less concerned with self-expression than with laying the groundwork for a revolutionary America.

In January 1919, before Reed's involvement in the dispute among left-wing Socialists over the formation of an American Communist party, he theorized about the kinds of changes needed to revolutionize the United States ("A New Appeal," *Revolutionary Age,* 18 January 1919). Obviously concerned about the conservatism of the American working class, he suggested that the American worker, ignoring the need for solidarity, "believes, consciously or unconsciously, that he can still rise above the working class, and above his fellows" (8). To make matters worse, those American workers who sought change tried to achieve it solely through political means without realizing the futility of their efforts. Since all branches of government were controlled by special interests, they were doomed to failure. Real change could only come about when workers took control of the nation's economic and political structure.

Reed was also troubled by the inability of either the labor movement or Socialist party to offer American workers an alternative to capitalism. The elitism and bread-and-butter approach of the American Federation of Labor merely perpetuated the inequities of the system. The Socialists were equally myopic. They seemed more intent on recreating a form of Jeffersonian democracy than on confronting the realities of the class structure. Even worse, the American Socialist party did not attract the workers. Ignoring working-class needs and interests, the party's ideology seemed geared more to foreign influences than American realities.

Reed wanted the left-wing Socialists to correct the failings of the American Socialist party. "They must find out from the *American workers* what they want most, and they must explain this in terms of the whole Labor Movement, and they must make the workers

want more—make them want the whole Revolution" (8). Like the
Bolsheviks, the left-wing Socialists would have to lead the workers
and express their wishes.

"A New Appeal" is one of Reed's most important articles because
it suggests a paradox in his thought. When engaged in disputes
over what an American Communist party should be, he always
argued that American communism should reflect the contours of
American history and the unique qualities of the American people.
He seemed to suggest a similar approach in "A New Appeal." But
as Theodore Draper suggests, when Reed ultimately submitted a
program for radical change, he fell back on a European model.[4] "My
idea is to make Socialists, and there is only one way of doing that—
by teaching Socialism, straight Socialism, revolutionary Socialism,
international Socialism. This is what the Russian Bolsheviki did;
this is what the German Spartacus group did" (8). No doubt Reed
fell back on what he knew best. His knowledge of Marx, the needs
of American workers, and the history of his own country were too
limited. He also had little experience in expressing a political ideology. After all, Reed was a poet who, more often than not, relied
on his senses in dealing with complex situations. Moreover, like
most American radicals then, he did not know exactly what could
be done to revolutionize a conservative work force or to combat the
power of the capitalist ethos. Reed was not enough of a theoretician
to Americanize his Marxism. He continued to waver between two
beliefs. A communist revolution in America might have to be patterned on the Bolshevik model or that model might have to be
altered in light of those qualities that made America unique.

A case in point is Reed's discussion of workers' control of industry.
In two articles written for the *Voice of Labor,* he described how
workers' control operated in the Soviet Union ("Shop Committees
in Russia," 15 August 1919; "Factory Control in Russia," 1 November 1919). In both articles Reed eulogizes while he describes,
in order to counter "lies" in the capitalist press "about 'lazy workmen' who spent all their time in talking when they should be
working" ("Shop Committees" 12). He claims that the factory committees kept the country going during the chaos of the Kerensky
regime. The problems they encountered then and after were those
created by counterrevolutionaries. In short, the workers took matters
into their own hands and capably operated industries throughout
the country.

The same thing had to happen in America if a revolution were to take place. Reed had spelled out what was to be done in an earlier article for the *Revolutionary Age* ("Workers' Control in America," 15 March 1919). American workers had to stop viewing themselves as merely cogs in the industrial process. Any hope for revolutionary change depended on their understanding the nature of the entire industrial operation. By understanding the production process they would better comprehend their own exploitation. Radical change would only come when a majority of workers were ready for it. The seizure of factories by individual groups of workers would be futile. Instead, committees of workers from all departments within a factory should be formed to examine the interdependency of the overall production process. Then, when the revolution came, American workers would not make the mistakes of their Russian counterparts who had demanded changes without knowing what the impact would be. American workers would also learn that skilled technicians and engineers would be needed to run the worker-controlled industries because of increased planning, efficiency, and propaganda.[5] In this piece, Reed was not defending worker control so much as trying to demonstrate how it could best be implemented in the United States. He was more candid and critical than in his *Voice of Labor* articles. Russian workers should be emulated, but their mistakes should not be duplicated. Under the most favorable circumstances, if workers did gain control of factories, they would need to exercise understanding and planning and exhibit revolutionary élan. There would have to be a long period of preparation. In this respect, the revolution Reed envisioned for America would be different from the one he witnessed in Russia.

"Why Political Democracy Must Go" was Reed's longest and most ambitious article of this period. It appeared in seven installments in the *New York Communist,* beginning in early May. The first five parts (8, 15, 24, 31 May; 7 June) described the failure of Populists, Progressives, workers, Socialists, and other would-be reformers to bring about change. In the last two parts (14, 21 June) he drew a Beardian sketch of wealthy men writing an elitist constitution and then dominating government to ensure their continuing power. Reed argued that reform efforts, the most radical ones included, had all failed because while reformers tried to change the political structure, they devoted scant attention to the question of who wielded the economic power.

This article reflected Reed's new interest in American history. Influenced by the economic interpretations of historians John Bach McMaster and Charles Beard, he tried to show the class biases within the American system of government that destroyed political democracy. As long as the American people accepted the capitalist ethos, fundamental change was impossible. Only when the illusions of political democracy were shattered could a just government function within the framework of a just economic system. "Property is power," he concluded. "Property is political power. Only the abolition of property will ensure the working of real democracy, and only the dictatorship of the proletariat can abolish property" (21 June, 7). Just as in Reed's article "Worker's Control in America," his intention here was didactic. The deceptions of political democracy had to be exposed. And this could be done by analyzing American history from a Marxist perspective.

Reed realized that his advocacy of a dictatorship of the proletariat in the place of political democracy would seem extreme to most Americans. He had briefly defended the idea in the spring of 1919, in an article on the IWW ("The I.W.W. and Bolshevism," *New York Communist*, 31 May 1919). While chiding the Wobblies for their lack of political activism, he also questioned their inability to see that a dictatorship of the proletariat was necessary only as long as capitalism existed. Later that summer he tried to place this concept in its revolutionary setting ("Aspects of the Russian Revolution," *Revolutionary Age*, 12 July 1919). He argued that no revolution, including the American, was ever carried out by a majority. A social revolution that challenged class rule could only be initiated by "a mass of class-conscious and resolute proletarians" who would then awaken "greater and greater masses of workers to an understanding of their interests" (10). The dictatorship that arose would lead the masses and anticipate their will through the workers' soviets. It was Marx grafted onto Rousseau, although Reed was vague on how the workers' will would operate. More important, as he showed in "A New Appeal," the European model was still the norm. Reed never implied that the United States could avoid the revolutionary necessity of a dictatorship of the proletariat. What he hoped to do in the article was to introduce American radicals to the idea of a workers' dictatorship. If they understood the concept, they would be more likely to accept it. But Reed never discussed what a dictatorship of the proletariat would be like in America. Would the

United States follow the Bolshevik lead, or would the revolution in America be different?

If Reed could not be pinned down on what he expected an American dictatorship to be, it was probably because he believed Americans should develop their own models. In one of his last articles he suggested once again that the workers' cause in America should not be blindly imitative of the Bolsheviks. In "Communism in America" (*Workers' Dreadnought*, 4 October 1919), an article he wrote as the bitter struggle over an American Communist party was going on, Reed argued that his faction, the Communist Labor party, exemplified the "natural growth from the old Socialist Party and represents what revolutionary forces there are in the Socialist movement of the United States" (3). To prepare the way for revolution, the Communist Labor party had absorbed all that was worthwhile in the American radical tradition, while the Communist party rejected it. Reed also pointed out that Communist party members included foreign-born workers and leaders who tried "to create a foreign working-class movement . . . organized along the lines of the Bolshevik Party in Russia (without any attempt to adapt it to the psychology of the American working-class) and ruled by the autocratic central committee of those foreign groups and by a few petit-bourgeois intellectuals who know nothing and care less about the American working-class and who have not amongst them a single man who can speak in simple language who can be understood by the workers in this country" (3). As in so many of his theoretical articles, Reed did not spell out how communism could be shaped to the American experience. At this point all he said was that an American Communist party would have to be creative and imitative, national as well as international in its orientation.

Much of the writing Reed did in 1919, especially those pieces for communist publications, differed considerably from most of his previous work. Ideology, history, and didacticism replace the humor and descriptive analysis that were his trademarks. Even the descriptive pieces that he wrote were meant to serve a purpose—either defending the Soviet Union or demonstrating the need for radical change in the United States. Yet in calling for revolution in America Reed was ambiguous about strategy. If the Russian or German models should not be copied, how would American communism differ? Would a revolutionary dictatorship be the same as that of the Bolsheviks? Would a conservative American working class respond to the class struggle? If foreign-born workers were more radical than their American counterparts, should they not form the nucleus of the revolutionary movement? Given the nature of American industry and trade unions, were workers' committees a possibility or a utopian dream? Reed confronted such questions in his writing and in his efforts to forge an American Communist party. When he left for Russia in the fall of 1919, he still had no clear answers. In fact, the same questions haunted him in the Soviet Union as he clashed with party dignitaries over ideologies. During this period, political concerns nearly controlled his life. And he had already, well before the advent of socialist realism, dedicated his art, at least for the time being, to the continuation of the class struggle.

Chapter Seven
Myth and Reality

At the time of his death Reed was indeed troubled, but his major concern was an old one. How could he write about what he wanted and, at the same time, support the revolution with his time and talents? This was a chronic problem for Reed, but never before had he faced it so intensely. Never before had he been so committed to a cause as he was to the Russian Revolution. Homesickness, the physical decline from his prison confinement in Finland, exasperation with party functionaries in Russia and America, all had something to do with his desire to return to New York to write the poems and books that he had put off for so long. Yet this desire reflected as well Reed's lifelong failure to balance a writing career with his activist impulses. When Louise Bryant came to Moscow in the fall of 1920, Reed was emerging from an intense period of commitment in which all his energies had flowed in but one direction. Now, in keeping with his pattern of the past, his thoughts turned to Croton, relaxation, and writing.

There is no way of knowing where Reed's career might have gone had he lived. Given the constant turmoil of his life, it is not likely that he would have resolved the tension between doing and writing. Nor would he have followed the path of two of his colleagues on the *Masses.* Floyd Dell gradually altered his radical beliefs as he tried to analyze rather than shape the world. Career and personal interests eventually superseded his commitment to radical social change. Cartoonist Robert Minor, who found it impossible to combine the life of an artist with that of a revolutionary, gave up his art for the Communist party. According to James B. Gilbert, Minor's "conflict between art and revolutionary politics was not due to the theoretical incompatibility of aesthetics and radical ideas, but to the attempt to live two different lives simultaneously."[1] While the debate over how revolutionary artists and writers should apportion their time continued for decades, it seems unlikely that Reed would have turned in either direction completely.[2] When Reed told Max Eastman that the class struggle played hell with his poetry, he was, in fact, acknowledging that his writing suffered from his activism. He tried while writing *Ten Days* to isolate himself completely from all political commitments to concentrate fully on his art. But during this same period he scolded Lincoln Steffens for his political apathy. As he chided his old friend and mentor for his inactivity, Reed was expressing his own fundamental view that writing alone could never be enough. In his own life he could never ease the tension between commitment to a cause and a career. And there was never any indication, especially in the turbulent years before his death, that he ever felt he could do so.

On a less personal level, Reed found another problem with the issue of "American exceptionalism."[3] He argued in several of his articles that America would have to find her own way to Marxism because of her unique historical and economic development. While Reed contradicted himself on just how this was to be done, he still sensed that blind imitation was not the remedy for radical social change at home. Radical intellectuals have debated the future of American Marxism for over half a century, and even though Reed at times argued both sides of the issue, he was among the first to confront it.

Reed's early death leaves us with some tantalizing questions about what he might have done had he lived. Did an expressed desire to return to writing poetry and fiction suggest a turning away from the kinds of propagandistic articles he had published in 1919? In returning to poetry would he have discovered a voice of his own? Would he have embraced the literary modernism and experimentation of the 1920s? As a party member, would he then have used his art to support the revolutionary cause? Reed had also been eager to write a novel based on his life. Could he have captured the uniqueness of his experiences or would this venture into fiction have been yet another period piece similar to Max Eastman's *Venture* or Harry Kemp's *More Miles?* And finally, in the projected *From Kornilov to Brest-Litovsk* could Reed have given life to portions of the revolution that he had not witnessed? It also is worth speculating on how changes in the Communist world would have influenced Reed's writing. What would have been his attitude towards Trotsky? Would the fight against fascism have been enough to offset the NEP, Stalin, or the Purge Trials? Would he have eventually fled like fellow journalist Louis Fischer from the gloom of the Russian purges to the idealism of the Republican cause in Spain? Or, like fellow radicals Agnes Smedley and Anna Louis Strong, would he have found an antidote for his radicalism in revolutionary China? Taken together, all these questions, as rhetorical as they may seem, simply underscore the tragic interruption of a most important literary career. Despite his shortened life, and remarkably so, John Reed left behind a body of work that insures his continuing significance as an American writer.

Many of the essays, plays, poems, stories, and books that Reed completed in a ten-year career, were written hastily, lacked depth, and suffered from inattention to careful craftmanship. In a career so torn between writing and acting this might have been the norm. But Reed was capable of greatness. His best work is noted for its uniquely honest qualities. The unaffected frankness of dialogue, the directness of presentation, and the careful attention to detail is reminiscent of Hemingway's later concern with simplicity and integrity in language and plot.[4] It was indeed Reed's social awareness as well as his honesty as a writer that led Hemingway's friend and traveling companion John Dos Passos to include a portrait of Reed in the second volume of his *U.S.A.* trilogy. The development of Reed's social conscience is the main theme of this brief sketch, but running throughout as a counterpointal refrain is Dos Passos's claim that "Reed was a Westerner and words meant what they said."[5] Recent critics argue that Reed's realistic, on-the-spot style of reporting helped pave the way for the documentary style of the 1930s.[6] Certainly the emotive impact and descriptive brilliance of his best writing enabled readers almost to feel or even experience the events they were reading about. Reed also tried to impose meaning on events he observed by trying to capture the emotions of the participants. His success often depended on the extent of his involvement or the strength of his commitment. In this way he set a standard for the new journalism of the 1960s. One of its great exponents, Norman Mailer, simply followed in Reed's footsteps when he described his adventures at the Pentagon in *Armies of the Night*.

At the time of his death Reed was still growing as a writer. His interests were catholic, but his genius lay in the expository narrative style that he used in his best articles and books. To some extent his genius also lay in being in the right place at the right time, but none of his books were simply the product of luck. Reed grew as a writer because he learned from his experiences, but, unlike his mentor Lincoln Steffens, he was incapable of detached observation.

This was one of the reasons he had so much trouble writing about the First World War. The war offered plenty of excitement and adventure, but he could not believe in it. This is why his best articles during this period reflect his antiwar views.

While Reed always seemed to have enormous confidence in his writing, his confidence as an observer developed more slowly. When he shared the commitments of the participants in Paterson and Mexico, a youthful Reed wrote as much about himself as about what he saw. His persona was never far from the center of activity, as though he was incapable of separating the two.[7] Not so in Russia. Still only thirty when he arrived in revolutionary Petrograd, Reed encountered an event so monumental, and, at times, so confusing, that it seemed to dwarf the participants. Rather than being overwhelmed, he was exhilarated. This time, instead of merely recording the progress of the revolution or his reaction to it, he grappled with its meaning. In *Ten Days,* Reed was always in the background. The Russian masses held center stage. Maturity and professional experience had something to do with his newfound confidence in himself as observer, but so too did his deeply felt empathy for the revolution. This was not an event used to assert his individuality. Rather, he used his writing skills to interpret the revolution and to support it.

It was this commitment to the revolutionary ethos, as personalized and idiosyncratic as it may have been, that set Reed apart from most of his contemporaries of Greenwich Village. Much like the nineteenth-century romantics, many of the artists and writers who shared Village life with Reed sought human liberation without challenging the basic economic and political institutions of their society. Not so John Reed whose identification with striking workers, Mexican peons, and Russian workers changed his life. The inequities of the world demanded major social reclamation, which seemed to Reed increasingly possible after he had observed the Bolshevik Revolution. As his political views changed, his writing did too. According to Raymond Williams, this is a common phenomenon. "To write in different ways is to live in different ways. It is also to be read in different ways, in different relations, and often by different people. This area of possibility, and thence of choice, is specific, not abstract, and commitment in its only important sense is specific in just these terms. It is specific within a writer's actual and possible social relations as one kind of producer. . . . Thus to recognize alignment is to learn, if we choose, the hard and total specifications of commitment."[8] To understand fully Reed's life and writing is to come to grips with the "hard and total specifications" of his commitments. He could not write well without them. Whereas a writer like Stephen Crane wrote best when he distanced himself from his subject, John Reed needed to identify with his. But his commitments had to be balanced against his creative ambitions, for they were forever in competition with his career and literary pursuits. Perhaps, then, it is the nature of this tension between acting and doing that helps explain the dynamics of his creativity as well as the limitations of his accomplishments.

Notes and References

Preface

1. Reed is Hilton Mann in Harry Kemp's novel *More Miles* (New York: Boni and Liveright, 1926); the main character, Jo Hancock, in Max Eastman's *Venture* (New York: A&C Boni, 1927); and Richard Lowell in Neith Boyce's *Constancy* in *The Folly of Others* (New York: Fox, Duffield & Co., 1904 [*sic*]).

2. James A. Michener, *The Bridge at Andau* (New York: Random House, 1957). The description appears in the dust jacket blurb.

3. Robert A. Rosenstone, *"Reds* As History," *Reviews in American History* (September 1982):308–10.

4. Walter Lippmann, "Legendary John Reed," *New Republic,* 26 December 1914, 16. In describing Reed as a perpetual playboy, Lippmann was retaliating for the stodgy manner he had been portrayed in Reed's playful *Day in Bohemia, or Life among the Artists.*

5. Albert Rhys Williams, *Journey into Revolution: Petrograd, 1917–1918* (Chicago: Quadrangle Books, 1969), 43.

6. "Almost Thirty," in *Adventures of a Young Man* (San Francisco: City Lights, 1975), 140.

Chapter One

1. Steffens to Mrs. C. J. Reed, 25 May 1932, in *The Letters of Lincoln Steffens,* 2 vols. (New York: Harcourt, Brace & Co., 1938), 2:921–22.

2. For the most complete history of the Reed family see Robert A. Rosenstone, *Romantic Revolutionary: A Biography of John Reed* (New York: Alfred A. Knopf, 1975), 7–22.

3. "Almost Thirty," in *Adventures of a Young Man,* 131. Further references follow in the text. A copy of the essay is also found in the John Reed Papers, Houghton Library, Harvard University. An edited version appeared in *New Republic,* 15 April 1936, 267–70.

4. Granville Hicks, *John Reed: The Making of a Revolutionary* (New York: Macmillan Co., 1937), 9.

5. *Morristown Alumnus,* n.d., p. 5, Morristown Archives, Morristown-Beard School, Morristown, N.J.

6. C. J. Reed to Thomas O. Brown, 5 November 1905, Morristown Archives.

7. C. J. Reed to Gentlemen, 19 September 1906, Morristown Archives.

8. Reed later embellished on the adventure for one of his earliest publications. John Reed and Julian Street, "Overboard," *Saturday Evening Post,* 28 October 1911, 15–17, 45–46.

9. Reed to Edward Eyre Hunt, 21 October 1910, Reed Papers.

10. Lincoln Steffens, *Autobiography* (New York: Harcourt, Brace, and Co., 1931), 653.

11. Hicks, *John Reed,* 65.

12. A copy of this article is found in the Reed Papers.

13. Steffens, *Autobiography,* 654.

14. Floyd Dell, *Homecoming: An Autobiography* (New York: Kennikat Press, 1969), 271–72.

15. Max Eastman, *Enjoyment of Living* (New York: Harper & Brothers, 1948), 406.

16. A number of books have been written examining the intellectual and cultural milieu of Village life. Three of the most recent are Leslie Fishbein, *Rebels in Bohemia* (Chapel Hill: University of North Carolina Press, 1982); Robert E. Humphrey, *Children of Fantasy* (New York: John Wiley & Sons, 1978); and Arthur Frank Wertheim, *The New York Little Renaissance* (New York: New York University Press, 1976). All three are well done, but none of them capture the ferment and fun of the Village as well as Rosenstone in his biography of Reed.

17. Reed to Eddy Hunt, 15 July 1912, Reed Papers.

18. Eastman, *Enjoyment of Living,* 523.

19. Reed to Edward Eyre Hunt, n.d. [in jail in Paterson], Reed Papers.

20. Hutchins Hapgood, *A Victorian in the Modern World* (New York: Harcourt, Brace and Co., 1939), 353.

21. Although Mabel Dodge Luhan, *Movers and Shakers,* vol. 3, *Intimate Memories* (New York: Harcourt, Brace, & Co., 1936), 188–89, claims to have originated the idea of a pageant, Rosenstone, *Romantic Revolutionary,* 126–27, questions her version of how the idea arose.

22. Joyce L. Kornbluh, *Rebel Voices: An IWW Anthology* (Ann Arbor: University of Michigan Press, 1964), 197–226, contains documents pertaining to the strike and the pageant.

23. Elizabeth Gurley Flynn, "The Truth About the Paterson Strike," in *Rebel Voices,* ed. Kornbluh, 221–22.

24. Dodge, *Movers and Shakers,* 217.

25. Reed to Hunt, n.d. (Arcetri, Italy), Reed Papers.

26. Reed to Hunt, 16 December 1913, Reed Papers.

27. Hicks, *John Reed,* 143.

28. *Metropolitan,* July 1914, 67.

29. Dunn's description of this incident is in the *New York Evening Post*, 27 February 1915.

30. Max Eastman, *Heroes I Have Known* (New York: Simon & Schuster, 1942), 213.

31. For a description of the O'Neill-Bryant affair see Doris Alexander, *The Tempering of Eugene O'Neill* (New York: Harcourt, Brace and World, 1962), 231–37, 242–44, 252–53.

32. U.S. Congress, House, Committee on Military Affairs, Hearings, 65th Cong., 1st sess., 14 April 1917.

33. Rosenstone, *Romantic Revolutionary,* 268–73.

34. Reed to Bryant, 11 June 1917, Reed Papers.

35. Reed to Bryant, 23 June 1917, Reed Papers.

36. Reed to Bryant, 4 July 1917, Reed Papers.

37. Reed to Bryant, 10 July 1917, Reed Papers.

38. Eastman, *Enjoyment of Living,* 566.

Chapter Two

1. Reed to Bryant, 8 July 1917, Reed Papers. All dates in this and subsequent chapters are from the Georgian rather than the Julian calendar, which was thirteen days earlier.

2. Reed to Robinson, 17 September 1917, Reed Papers.

3. Williams, *Journey into Revolution,* 43–63.

4. Ibid., 30.

5. Ibid., 41.

6. Russian Notebooks, Reed Papers.

7. Reed to Robinson, 16 October 1917, Reed Papers.

8. *Ten Days That Shook the World* (New York: Boni & Liveright, 1919), 50–51. Further references follow in the text.

9. Louise Bryant, *Six Red Months in Russia* (New York: George H. Doran, 1918), 202; Also see John Reed, "On Intervention in Russia," *Liberator,* November 1918, 15; "How Soviet Russia Captures Imperial Germany," *Liberator,* January 1919, 19–21.

10. Williams, *Journey into Revolution,* 224.

11. Ibid., 199.

12. Rosenstone, *Romantic Revolutionary,* 289.

13. Williams, *Journey into Revolution,* 201–2.

14. Edgar Sisson, *One Hundred Red Days* (New Haven: Yale University Press, 1931), 256–58, footnoted the speeches of Reed and Williams as reported in *Izvestia.*

15. Rosenstone, *Romantic Revolutionary,* 314.

16. Arno Dosch-Fluerot, "World Man Tells of Reed in Russia," New York *World,* 19 October 1920.

17. Williams, *Journey into Revolution,* 221–32.

18. Max Eastman, *Love and Revolution* (New York: Random House, 1964), 69–78.

19. Hicks, *John Reed,* 305–7.

20. Melvyn Dubofsky, *We Shall Be All* (New York: Quandrangle/New York Times Book Co., 1969), 433–37.

21. Eastman, *Love and Revolution,* 109.

22. Ibid., 106.

23. *New York Times,* 14 and 15 September 1918.

24. Art Young, *On My Way* (New York: H. Liveright, 1928), 293.

25. Eastman, *Love and Revolution,* 119. See also Transcript of John Reed, *USA v. The Masses Publishing Company, et al.,* 3 October 1918, United States District Court, Southern District of New York, in Granville Hicks Papers, George Arents Research Library, Syracuse University, Syracuse, New York.

26. U.S. Congress, Senate, Subcommittee on the Judiciary, *Brewing and Liquor Interests and German and Bolshevik Propaganda: Report and Hearings,* 66th Cong., 1st sess., 20 February 1919, 465–561. Testimony by Louise Bryant.

27. Ibid, 21 February 1919, 561–601. Testimony by John Reed.

28. Rosenstone, *Romantic Revolutionary,* 345.

29. *New York Times,* 7 April 1919.

30. Eastman, *Heroes I Have Known,* 223.

31. Lincoln Steffens, "A Letter about Jack Reed," *New Republic,* 20 May 1936, 50.

32. James Weinstein, *The Decline of Socialism in America: 1912–1925* (New York: Viking Press, 1967), 177–233; Theodore Draper, *The Roots of American Communism* (New York: Viking Press 1957), 97–196.

33. Art Young, *His Life and Times* (New York: Sheridan House, 1939), 363.

34. Reed to Bryant, 21 October 1919, Reed Papers.

35. Reed to Bryant, 9 November 1919, Reed Papers.

36. Angelica Balabanoff, *John Reed—Poet and Revolutionist,* undated pamphlet, Reed Papers; Elizabeth Drabkina, "I Knew John Reed," *New World Review* 36 (Winter-Fall 1968):19–20.

37. Emma Goldman, *Living My Life,* 2 vols. (New York: A.A. Knopf, 1931), 2:740.

38. Eadmonn MacAlpine, Account of Finnish Arrest, Written for Louise Bryant (1934), typescript, Reed Papers.

39. Reed to Bryant, 3 May 1920, Reed Papers.

40. Reed to Bryant, 15 May 1920, Reed Papers.

41. Reed to Bryant, 2 June 1920, Reed Papers.

42. Rosenstone, *Romantic Revolutionary,* 374–77.

43. Jane Degras, ed., *The Communist International, 1919–1943, Documents* (New York: Oxford University Press, 1956), 1:398.

44. Angelica Balabanoff, "John Reed's Last Days," *Modern Monthly,* January 1937, 3–6; *My Life as a Rebel* (New York: Harper and Brothers, 1968), 243–46, 274–75.

45. Reed Papers.

46. Balabanoff, *My Life as a Rebel,* 281–82, 291–92. Benjamin Gitlow, *The Whole of Their Lives* (New York: Charles Scribner's Sons, 1948), 33–36. Gitlow's book is written from the viewpoint of an ex-Communist, is filled with errors, and must be used cautiously.

47. Louise Bryant, "Last Days With John Reed," *Liberator,* February 1921, 11.

48. Ibid.; Bryant to Margaret G. Reed, 20 October 1920, Reed Papers.

49. Clare Sheridan, *Mayfair to Moscow* (New York: Boni and Liveright, 1921), 162.

50. Emma Goldman, *My Further Disillusionment in Russia* (New York: Doubleday, Page & Co., 1924), 24–26; Balabanoff, "John Reed's Last Days," 3–6; Marguerite E. Harrison, *Marooned in Moscow* (New York: George H. Doran, 1921), 220–23. Draper, *Roots of American Communism,* 284–93, goes into the most detail analyzing the contradictory views of Reed's disillusionment.

51. Virginia Gardner, *Friend and Lover: The Life of Louise Bryant* (New York: Horizon Press, 1982), 301–6.

52. Rosenstone, *Romantic Revolutionary,* 379.

53. Williams, *Journey into Revolution,* 320.

Chapter Three

1. Drabkina, "I Knew John Reed," 20, 22.

2. Bryant to Margaret G. Reed, 20 October 1920, Reed Papers.

3. "The Best Camping Experience," Unpublished Manuscripts, Reed Papers.

4. Malcolm Cowley, *Exile's Return: A Literary Odyssey of the 1920s* (New York: Viking Press, 1966), 16.

5. Quoted in Hicks, *John Reed,* 23. Several of Reed's early poems and stories that he wrote for the *Morristonian* have been lost. I am deeply indebted to Robert Rosenstone for providing me with copies of stories and poems that I was unable to locate in the Morristown Archives or in other Reed repositories. For a fascinating discussion of the martial ideal and "cult of experience" that permeated the America of Reed's youth, see T. J. Jackson Lears, *No Place of Grace: Antimodernism and the Transformation of American Culture 1880–1920* (New York: Pantheon Books, 1981), 117–39.

6. This poem is found in John Reed, *Collected Poems of John Reed,* ed. Corliss Lamont (Westport, Conn.: Lawrence Hill & Co., 1985), 8.

The collection contains a number of poems Reed published at Morristown, Harvard, and in various magazines, as well as over two dozen unpublished poems. It also includes *The Day in Bohemia, or Life among the Artists*. Except for poems written at Morristown, Reed's published poetry as well as several unpublished poems are found in John Reed, *The Complete Poetry of John Reed*, ed. Jack Alan Robbins (Washington, D.C.: University Press of America, 1983). Unless otherwise indicated future references to Reed's poetry will be to this volume.

7. Robert Hallowell, "John Reed," *New Republic,* 17 November 1920, 298.

8. Hicks, *John Reed,* 48.

9. Quoted in J. Donald Adams, *Copey of Harvard: A Biography of Charles Townsend Copeland* (Boston: Houghton Mifflin, 1960), 167.

10. *Tit for Tat,* Unpublished Manuscripts, Reed Papers.

11. A thirty-five-page typescript of *Diana's Debut* is found in the Reed Papers.

12. *The Last of the Pirates,* Unpublished Manuscripts, Reed Papers.

13. In Reed Papers.

14. Reed to Harriet Monroe, 11 September 1912, in *Poetry* 17 (January 1921):209.

15. Christopher Wilson has been kind enough to allow me to read his fascinating analysis of the ways in which he believes Reed attempted to transform a primitive, antimodern literary interest to the idiom of urban existence. "Broadway Nights: John Reed and the City" (Paper delivered at the American Studies Association Convention, San Diego, Calif., 3 November 1985).

16. Harriet Monroe, *A Poet's Life* (New York: Macmillan, 1938), 390.

17. Steffens, *Autobiography,* 690.

18. Quoted in Susan Glaspell, *The Road to the Temple* (New York: Frederick A. Stokes Co., 1927), 302.

19. Wertheim, *The New York Little Renaissance,* 244.

20. Steffens to Reed, 1 March 1911, in *Letters,* 1:265–66.

21. Steffens to Reed, 6 April 1911, Reed Papers.

22. "The Harvard Renaissance," seventy-three-page typescript, 1912, 45, Reed Papers.

23. "Art For Art's Sake," three-page typescript, 1912, 3, Reed Papers.

24. See Rosenstone, *Romantic Revolutionary,* 89. The story is included in a collection of Reed's stories, *Adventures of a Young Man*.

25. In an unpublished short story entitled "Success," Reed papers, he wrote: "I admit that when anyone writes a story about the voice of the city he is poaching on the preserves of O. Henry" (1). Also in his chance meeting with William James (*American,* November 1911) both he and the

philosopher agreed upon their mutual admiration for the New York storyteller.

Chapter Four

1. Hicks, *John Reed,* 91.

2. The first collection of Reed's stories was assembled by a colleague on the *Masses,* Floyd Dell: *Daughter of the Revolution,* (New York: Vanguard Press, 1927). There are two other collections: *The Education of John Reed,* ed. John Stuart (New York: International Publishers, 1955), contains several of his best-known stories, articles, and poems, and *Adventures of a Young Man.*

3. Daniel Aaron, *Writers on the Left* (1961; reprint ed., New York: Harcourt, Brace & World, 1977), briefly discusses Crane's influence on Reed. But a more detailed discussion of the Crane influence is in Wilson, "Broadway Nights."

4. The only important pieces about Mexico not included in *Insurgent Mexico* are: "Mac-American" (*Masses,* April 1914), and a brief sketch of Pancho Villa, "With Villa in Mexico" (*Metropolitan,* February 1914). Unless otherwise indicated all quotations from *Insurgent Mexico* are from the edition published by D. Appleton & Co. (New York: 1914).

5. "Insurgent Mexico," *Outlook,* 21 October 1914, 440.

6. Rosenstone, *Romantic Revolutionary,* 167.

7. Mexican Notebooks, Reed Papers.

8. Ibid.

9. Steffens to Reed, 19 November 1914, in *Letters,* 1:350.

10. Gregory Mason, "Reed, Villa and the Village," *Outlook,* 6 May 1935, 1.

11. In writing this article Reed hired an assistant, Fred Boyd, to assist with the research. Rosenstone, *Romantic Revolutionary,* 167.

12. *The War in Eastern Europe* (New York: Charles Scribner's Sons, 1916), v. Unless otherwise indicated all subsequent quotations are from this edition. Scribner's later published an abridged edition of the book in 1919.

13. "Here and There in Europe," *Independent,* 5 June 1916, 401.

14. Rosenstone, *Romantic Revolutionary,* 232.

15. Ibid., 166.

16. H. C. Peterson, *Propaganda for War: The Campaign against American Neutrality, 1914–1917* (Norman: University of Oklahoma Press, 1939), 139.

17. A copy of *The Eternal Quadrangle* is in the Reed Papers.

18. A copy of *Enter Dibble* is in the Reed Papers.

19. A copy of *Everymagazine* is in the Beinecke Rare Book and Manuscript Library, Yale University, New Haven, Conn. Citations are from this text.

20. *Freedom* is included in two collections: *The Provincetown Plays*, 2d ser. (New York: n.p., 1916), and *A Treasury of Plays for Men*, ed. Frank Shay, (Boston: n.p., 1923). Citations in this chapter are from the Shay edition.

21. Helen Deutsch and Stella Hanau, *The Provincetown: A Story of The Theatre* (New York: Farrar and Rinehart, 1931), 32–33.

22. Hapgood, *A Victorian in the Modern World*, 354.

Chapter Five

1. Reed to Robinson, 17 September 1917, Reed Papers.

2. The poem was ultimately published in the *New Masses*, 15 October 1935. I have quoted from the Robbins's edition of Reed's poetry.

3. George F. Kennan, "The Sisson Documents," *Journal of Modern History* 27 (June 1956):130–54.

4. Reed still was not comfortable with the language and his efforts at translation can be observed on the backs of many of the documents he brought out of Russia now in the Reed Papers.

5. John Howard Lawson, Introduction to *Ten Days That Shook the World* (New York: International Publishers, 1967), xii–xiii. Another, less convincing analysis of Reed's structural intentions is Harry Henderson III, "John Reed's Urban Comedy of Revolution," *Massachusetts Review* 14 (Spring 1973):421–35, in which he argues that Reed approached the revolutionary class struggle as a kind of elaborate comedy of manners.

6. Reed's guilt-ridden statement to Williams, *Journey into Revolution*, 41, about the nature of their radicalism suggests that Paterson was still very much on his mind. In Paterson the workers had, in part, failed because of their dependence on intellectuals like Williams and Reed.

7. Untitled and undated typescript in Reed Papers.

8. Robert V. Daniels, *Red October: The Bolshevik Revolution of 1917* (Boston: Beacon Press, 1984), 74–77, describes this important meeting. See also the 1967 International Publishers' edition of *Ten Days*, n. 38, 374–75.

9. Joseph North, "Reportage," in *The American Writers Congress*, ed. Henry Hart (New York: International Publishers, 1935), 121.

10. Harold Stearns, "The Unending Revolution," *Dial*, 22 March 1919, 302, first commented on Reed's use of ellipses and proposed that they were a "happy incorporation of the technique of Wellsian suggestiveness."

11. The 1967 International Publishers' edition of *Ten Days* contains one of the most thorough jobs of editing Reed's mistakes.

12. Daniels, *Red October*, 119–20.

13. Ibid.

14. Williams, *Journey into Revolution*, 139–42, explains what actually happened.

15. Donald Pizer, "Documentary Narrative As Art: William Manchester and Truman Capote," in *The Reporter as Artist: A Look at the New Journalism Controversy,* ed. Ronald Weber (New York: Hastings House, 1974), 209.

16. William Stotts, *Documentary Expression and Thirties America* (New York: Oxford University Press, 1976), 11.

17. Ibid., 300–305.

18. Balabanoff, *My Life as a Rebel,* 177.

19. The 1922 edition by Boni & Liveright (New York) was the first to include Lenin's remarks, which are now found in most editions of *Ten Days.*

20. Draper, *Roots of American Communism,* 115.

21. Goldman, *Living My Life,* 2:684.

22. Daniels, *Red October,* 251.

23. A. J. P. Taylor, Introduction to *Ten Days That Shook the World* (1977; reprint ed. New York: Penguin, 1981), vii.

24. George Kennan, *Russia Leaves the War* (New York: Praeger, 1967), 68–69.

25. *New York Times,* 27 April 1919.

26. "Ten Days that Shook the World," *New Republic,* 31 May 1919, 158.

27. Stearns, "The Unending Revolution," 301–2.

28. *Athenaeum,* 15 August 1919, 768.

Chapter Six

1. Eastman, *Heroes I Have Known,* 208.

2. David M. Kennedy, *Over Here: The First World War and American Society* (New York: Oxford University Press, 1980), 67; Robert K. Murray, *Red Scare: A Study in National Hysteria, 1919–1920* (Minneapolis: University of Minnesota Press, 1955), 85–86.

3. Hicks, *John Reed,* 353.

4. Draper, *Roots of American Communism,* 136–37.

5. It is unknown whether or not Reed had read Thorstein Veblen. The need for engineers to oversee the entire production process certainly smacks of the great debunker.

Chapter Seven

1. James B. Gilbert, *Writers and Partisans: A History of Literary Radicalism in America* (New York: Wiley, 1968), 84.

2. For an interesting analysis of this ongoing debate see Aaron, *Writers on the Left,* and Richard Pells, *Radical Visions and American Dreams: Culture and Social Thought in the Depression Years* (New York: Harper and Row, 1973).

3. John P. Diggins, *The American Left in the Twentieth Century* (New York: Harcourt, Brace, Jovanovich, 1973), 95.

4. I am indebted to Robert Rosenstone for first suggesting the similarities between the two writers.

5. John Dos Passos, *1919* (1932), in *U.S.A.* (1938; reprint ed. Boston: Houghton Mifflin, 1960), 10–14.

6. Gilbert, *Writers and Partisans,* 13–14; Fishbein, *Rebels in Bohemia,* 182–83. For a skillful discussion of the documentary style of the 1930s, see Stotts, *Documentary Expression and Thirties America,* 5–45.

7. The cult of experience can easily degenerate into narcissism as Christopher P. Wilson argues in *The Labor of Words: Literary Professionalism in the Progressive Era* (Athens: University of Georgia Press, 1985), 198.

8. Raymond Williams, *Marxism and Literature* (Oxford: Oxford University Press, 1977), 205.

Selected Bibliography

PRIMARY SOURCES

The John Reed Papers at the Houghton Library, Harvard University, contain many of Reed's unpublished works, which are invaluable in tracing his development as a writer. Those who wish to examine the entire body of Reed's works should consult the bibliography in Granville Hicks, *John Reed: The Making of a Revolutionary*. The majority of Reed's magazine articles are in the *Metropolitan* (July 1913–May 1916), the *Masses* (June 1914–November-December 1917), the *Liberator* (March 1918–August 1919), and the *Revolutionary Age* (December 1918–August 1919). Most of his signed newspaper articles are in the New York *World* (1 March 1914–26 December 1915), and the *New York Mail* (25 May 1917–9 August 1917). For titles and sources of uncollected works, magazines, and newspaper articles, see Index under "Reed, John; Works."

1. Books and Pamphlets
The Causes behind Mexico's Revolution. Introduction by John Bates Clark. New York: American Association for International Conciliation, 1914.
Insurgent Mexico. New York: D. Appleton & Co., 1914. Reprint. New York: Simon & Schuster, 1969.
The Sisson Documents. New York: Liberator Publishing Co., 1918.
Ten Days That Shook the World. New York: Boni & Liveright, 1919. Reprints. New York: Boni & Liveright, 1922, with a foreword by V. I. Lenin; International Publishers, 1926; Random House, 1934, 1960, with an introduction by Bertram Wolfe; New American Library, 1967, with an introduction by Granville Hicks; International Publishers, 1967, with a preface by N. K. Krupskaya and an introduction by John Howard Lawson; Penguin Books, 1977, 1981, with an introduction by A. J. P. Taylor.
The War in Eastern Europe. New York: Charles Scribner's Sons, 1916. Abridged ed., 1919.

2. Collected Stories and Articles
Adventures of a Young Man: Short Stories from Life. Introduction by Lawrence Ferlinghetti. San Francisco: City Lights, 1975.
Daughter of the Revolution. Edited by Floyd Dell. New York: Vanguard Press, 1927.

The Education of John Reed: Selected Writings. Edited with an introduction
by John Stuart. New York: International Publishers, 1955.

3. Plays and Skits
Diana's Debut [by J. S. Reed]. Music by Walter S. Langshaw. Boston:
White-Smith Co., 1910.
Everymagazine: An Immorality Play. Music by Bill Daly. New York: pri-
vately printed, 1913.
Freedom. In *The Provincetown Plays,* 2d ser. New York: n.p., 1916. In *A
Treasury of Plays for Men.* Edited by Frank Shay. Boston: n.p., 1923.
Moondown. Masses, September 1913, pp. 8–9.
The Peace That Passeth Understanding. Liberator, March 1919, pp. 25, 28–
29, 30–31.

4. Books of Verse and Collected Poetry
Collected Poems. Edited with a foreword by Corliss Lamont. Westport,
Conn.: Lawrence Hill & Company, 1985.
The Complete Poetry of John Reed. Edited by Jack Alan Robbins. With an
introduction by Granville Hicks. Washington, D.C.: University Press
of America, 1983.
The Day in Bohemia, or Life among the Artists. Riverside, Conn.: privately
printed, 1913.
Tamburlaine. Riverside, Conn.: Frederick C. Bursch, 1917.

SECONDARY SOURCES

Aaron, Daniel. *Writers on the Left.* 1961. Reprint. New York: Harcourt,
Brace & World, 1977. Traces Reed's relationship to the American
radical movement in the early twentieth century and suggests that
he followed in the footsteps of Jack London.
Bryant, Louise. *Six Red Months in Russia.* New York: George H. Doran,
1918. Although there is relatively little about Reed in the book, it
is interesing to compare Bryant's straightforward, journalistic ap-
proach with *Ten Days.*
Cheuse, Alan. *The Bohemians: John Reed & His Friends Who Shook the World.*
Cambridge: Apple-Wood Books, 1973. The novel Reed never wrote.
Magnifies his romantic rather than political activities.
Diggins, John P. *The American Left in the Twentieth Century.* New York:
Harcourt Brace Jovanovich, 1973. Reed as the committed poet-play-
boy of the "Lyrical Left" who left no important legacy to future
generations of American radicals.
Draper, Theodore. *The Roots of American Communism.* New York: Viking

Press, 1957. Thoroughly analyzes the question of Reed's disillusionment, and traces his efforts to help organize an American Communist party.

Duke, David C. *Distant Obligations: Modern American Writers and Foreign Causes.* New York: Oxford University Press, 1983. Places Reed in the context of other American writers who have voluntarily participated in foreign causes.

Eastman, Max. *Enjoyment of Living.* New York: Harper & Brothers, 1948. Material on Eastman and Reed's friendship and work on the *Masses* until around 1916.

————. *Heroes I Have Known: Twelve Who Lived Great Lives.* New York: Simon & Schuster, 1942. Written after Eastman had broken with communism and stresses Reed's disillusionment with the revolution.

————. *Love and Revolution: My Journey through an Epoch.* New York: Random House, 1964. Eastman's memoirs of the 1917–41 period including his and Reed's activities on the *Masses* and *Liberator.*

Fishbein, Leslie. *Rebels in Bohemia: The Radicals of the Masses, 1911–1917.* Chapel Hill: University of North Carolina Press, 1982. An indictment of the *Masses* radicals for lacking a sustaining ideology devoted to social change. Argues, mistakenly I believe, that Reed, the exception, had abandoned his art for the revolution.

Gardner, Virginia. *"Friend and Lover": The Life of Louise Bryant.* New York: Horizon Press, 1982. Meticulously researched study that documents Bryant's courage but sometimes overemphasizes her literary abilities and feminist commitments.

Gelb, Barbara. *So Short A Time: A Biography of John Reed and Louise Bryant.* New York: W. W. Norton & Co., 1973. An impressionistic, romanticized narrative lacking in critical analysis and marred by factual errors.

Giffin, Frederick C. *Six Who Protested: Radical Opposition to the First World War.* New York: Kennikat Press, 1977. A brief summary of Reed's opposition to the war that covers no new ground.

Hicks, Granville. *John Reed: The Making of a Revolutionary.* New York: Macmillan Co., 1937. A masterfully researched biography with a detailed bibliography of Reed's works, but it ultimately fails to capture Reed's essence because it overemphasizes the political side of his personality.

Hovey, Tamara. *John Reed: Witness to Revolution.* Los Angeles: George Sand Books, 1982. Little new in this brief biography, except for Reed's relationship with Carl Hovey, editor of the *Metropolitan.*

Humphrey, Robert E. *Children of Fantasy: The First Rebels of Greenwich Village.* New York: John Wiley & Sons, 1978. Five biographical sketches, including one of Reed, that stress the Villagers' preoccupation with self-gratification rather than social revolution.

Luhan, Mabel Dodge. *Movers and Shakers.* Vol. 3, *Intimate Memories.* New York: Harcourt, Brace, 1936. Luhan's reminiscences about her relationship with Reed and their involvement in the Paterson Pageant.

O'Connor, Richard, and Walker, Dale L. *The Lost Revolutionary: A Biography of John Reed.* New York: Harcourt, Brace & World, 1967. Written from a cold war perspective. Neither Reed nor his revolutionary activities are taken seriously.

O'Neill, William L., ed. *Echoes of Revolt: "The Masses" 1911–1917.* Introduction by Irving Howe. Afterword by Max Eastman. Chicago: Quadrangle Books, 1966. A brief history of the *Masses* with selections from the magazine, including several of Reed's contributions.

Rosenstone, Robert A. *Romantic Revolutionary: A Biography of John Reed.* New York: Alfred A. Knopf, 1975. A truly outstanding biography that captures the uniqueness of Reed as well as the temper of his era.

Wertheim, Arthur Frank. *The New York Little Renaissance: Iconoclasm, Modernism, and Nationalism in American Culture, 1908–1917.* New York: New York University Press, 1976. Among the Village groups revolting against the genteel tradition, Reed and his *Masses* associates are described as the most concerned with social change.

Williams, Albert Rhys. *Journey into Revolution: Petrograd, 1917–1918.* Edited by Lucita Williams. Foreword by Josephine Herbst. Chicago: Quadrangle Books, 1969. Fellow participant with Reed during the Bolshevik Revolution. Williams's recollections are invaluable in recapturing his and Reed's activities and enthusiasms.

Index

DATE DUE

DEMCO 38-297